HAWAIIAN REEF FiSH

THE IDENTIFICATION BOOK

CASEY MAHANEY

SPECIAL ACKNOWLEDGMENTS

Only with the help of the following people was I able to complete this book. I would like to acknowledge them for their contribution to this book.

Astrid Witte: Astrid was my inspiration during the many months it took to complete this book. Astrid assisted in the writing, editing, research, photography, cataloging of slides and the feeding of the author. Without her knowledge, organization and patience I would not have been able to complete this book. Astrid provided me much needed insight for composing a complete and accurate resource for divers and snorkelers.

Steve Mahaney: It was my brother Steve who gave me my first job in the dive industry in 1983. Since then we have worked together teaching scuba diving to thousands of people. It was Steve who encouraged me to take up underwater photography and who suggested that I write this book. He also assisted in the writing of some of the text and marketing ideas.

My parents: Lois and Jack Mahaney. My appreciation goes way beyond the scope of this book. They have always supported my many endeavors, from a college education to me moving to Hawaii. Without their support and foresight none of this would have been possible. Their enthusiasm and financial support has again allowed a dream turn to reality. If not for them this book would still be on the computer.

Sue Davis of Graphic Services: I feel very lucky to have found Sue. She was the spark plug this project needed. Sue provided not only enthusiasm, but the much needed expertise that was required to prepare not only the book for printing, but also myself. Sue tirelessly provided me with information, connections and ideas during the final stages of completion. Sue is one of those rare people who gives you way more than you pay for.

Astrid Witte contributed approximatly one third of the photos in this book.

Gui Garcia contributed photos seen on pages: 47/c, 53/a, 99/a.

TABLE OF CONTENTS

READ FIRST: INCLUDES INTRODUCTION ON HOW TO USE THIS BOOK AND BASIC FISH IDENTIFICATION TECHNIQUES. 4

HOW IT BEGAN: WHERE THE ISLANDS CAME FROM, HOW THE FISH GOT HERE. 6

INTRODUCTION

Inspired by the need for a more complete and organized identification source this volume focuses on identifying both the common and uncommon reef fish found in Hawaiian waters. The book is structured in an easy to read format that organizes information along side each photo. This will allow you to quickly acquire specific information such as:

COMMON NAME: Often more than one. *Hawaiian Names* are listed next to the photo when available. The Hawaiians seemed to only name the fish they used as a food source.

SCIENTIFIC NAME: Used to cross reference common names.

FAMILY: Both the Common and Scientific. Common name also listed next to the photo.

AVERAGE SIZE: At maturity

DIET: Food most commonly eaten.

DEPTH FOUND: Most fish perfer certain depth ranges, but this can vary. Remember the fish can't read.

HABITAT and BEHAVIOR: This category is designed to give the fish watcher information on the most likely habitat the species is commonly found in. **Behavior** will also aid in identification.

DISTRIBUTION: Some fish are only found in Hawaii. (Endemic). Most of the reef fish can also be found in other parts of the worlds oceans. *SEE DISTRIBUTION AREAS*

*The photo*s that follow will show you the basic colors and shape of the subject. Keep in mind that all fish go through different color phases based on maturity and current behavior. For example, the Yellowtail Coris, as a juvenile is red with white spots. As it matures, it goes through many color changes so that when it reaches adulthood, it is a combination of red, green, yellow, and blue. Some fish will take on a slightly different shade of color while engaging in certain activities, such as feeding, being cleaned or courting. So look beyond the color of the fish in your efforts to identify it; check out its behavior and habitat on the reef. Also, take a look at fin placement. It is another important key to identification.

On the pages that follow I have focused attention not only on the most commonly seen reef fish, but also on the fish that are usually only seen by the investigative SCUBA divers.

Basic Coral identification is included due to its importance in building the foundation of the reef ecosystem. Coral is the basis of the reef, and without it there would be no means to support a reef fish population.

All of these *photos* were taken of the fish in their natural surroundings, with special concern in regards to the subjects sensitivity. In the past, underwater photographers have been notorious for disturbing the reef when it came to "getting the photo;" frequently moving subjects to the perfect background has been a standard practice. I avoid this because it not only stresses the animal, it can also disrupt their feeding patterns and often exposes the animal to danger from other predators. I would like to emphasis the preservation of the ecosystem by raising the consciousness level of all visitors to the underwater world.

This book is devoted to a future of ecologically sound methods for observing, photographing, and interacting with the marine environment in its *natural* setting; with special emphasis on making your presence a quiet and gentle one.

DISTRIBUTION AREAS

Indo Pacific: Covers the ocean area from the Indian ocean to east of the Hawaiian Islands. This includes the Red Sea, the Islands of Polynesia, Philippines, Micronesia, Easter Island and the Hawaiian archipelago.

Western Pacific: This is a subcategory of the Indo Pacific that specifically covers the Islands of Indonesia, The Philippines, and Australia this area reaches eastward to be bordered by the Islands of Micronesia and the Island of Polynesia.

Central Pacific: Encompasses the area surrounding the Islands of Micronesia.

Indo - Pan - Pacific Includes the Indo Pacific and along the coast of Central America (Panama).

All other distribution areas are self explanatory.
Example: Red Sea or Endemic to Hawaii

HOW IT BEGAN

Over 70 million years ago, far beneath the ocean, a *"hotspot"* on the ocean floor began spewing lava into the sea. 43 million years later (give or take a day), the lava reached 18,000 feet upward to begin forming a series of seamounts that we now call the Hawaiian Archipelago. This process is still continuing today and, as I write this book, lava is still building the Big Island of Hawaii a mere 50 miles away from where I sit. As each Hawaiian Island was formed, it "floated" upon the Earth's mantle and drifted away to make room for the next one. Consequently, Kauai, the northernmost main island is dominated by ancient, extinct volcanoes and is estimated to be about 5 million years old. Hawaii Island, on the other hand, is still very active and geologists estimate its age to be less that 1 million years.

The Hawaiian Islands are the most isolated islands in the world. Due to their isolation, the evolution of animal and plant life has been greatly restricted. Most of the terrestrial plants and animals were brought by man. The marine life, however, has been dependent on ocean currents. Unfortunately the prevailing currents don't favor dispersal of marine life to Hawaii to the same degree that they support the other parts of the Pacific. The Western Pacific is considered by scientists to be the dispersal center for tropical marine life which begins in a larval stage and drifts around in the open sea as plankton. The length of time spent in this planktonic stage, along with the strength and direction of currents determines the organism's final destination. As you move eastward across the Pacific you will find a decrease in the number of aquatic species. Experts estimate the fish population to be approximately 2000 species in the Philippines, 1000 in Micronesia, and 450 in Hawaii.

As a result of isolation, the Hawaiian Islands' marine habitat has benefited from a unique evolution over time. Through interbreeding, Hawaiian reefs have produced a number of endemic species. About 30% of the fish are found no where else in the world. The investigative snorkeler or diver will find an incredible variety of unique marine life in Hawaii. Although lacking in soft coral, Hawaiian reefs make up for it in sensational underwater volcanic geology. Divers can expect to see spectacular archway formations, caverns, and lava tubes. These "tubes" are like underwater tunnels and most of them boast skylights that tend to create dazzling solar powered light displays when the sun is at the right angle. *Then, there are the fish.....* Stunning hues and astonishing shapes that make the reef look like colors in motion.

For SCUBA divers I recommend you carry a small dive light so you can see the hidden treasures concealed within the crevices of the reef. Remember, almost everything you see on the reef is **ALIVE** so observe quietly and try not to disrupt anything. Besides, some things *"DO"* touch back

CORAL REEF FACTS

Coral reefs are built from a symbiotic relationship between coral and an algae called zooxanthellae. The growth rate is dependent on the amount of sunlight that this special algae receives. Abundant sunlight promotes algae growth which in turn leads to a rapid development of the coral's calcareous skeleton. It takes thousands of years for large reefs to develop. Once the coral takes a firm hold then other marine life can find food and shelter, thus, beginning to inhabit the resulting nooks and crannies.

As visitors to this aquatic wonderland, it is important to have a basic understanding of the coral reef in order to comprehend the behavior of fish and their complex inter-relationships. Some corals thrive in shallow surging water, others like the deeper, calm water. Most of the corals found in Hawaii, with a couple of exceptions, are hard encrusting reef building corals.

On the fragile reef, we as scuba divers or snorkelers, owe a responsibility to nature. Observe, but do not destroy or deplete. Touching a piece of coral damages the outer layer and makes it susceptible to disease or attack from other organisms. Fortunately the public is becoming more and more aware that we have to protect this precious resource. Use of permanent moorings, so boats don't have to drop anchor, is becoming common. Scuba divers are learning, through better instruction, the importance of buoyancy control and how to avoid accidentally (or ignorantly) coming in contact with the reef.

By increasing our knowledge and awareness of the oceans' fragility we are able to preserve this precious treasure for the future generations. Since coral is the building block of the reef, protection must begin with preserving the coral.

COMMON NAME: Antler Coral

SCIENTIFIC NAME: Pocillopora eydouxi

AVERAGE SIZE: 3-5ft across.

FAMILY: Coral - Pocillopora

DIET: Nutrients provided by sunlight and algae.

DEPTH FOUND: 25-70ft.

HABITAT: Prefers water below the surge zone. Home to many fish and crustaceans. Resembles cauliflower coral but is much larger. Look for damselfishes.

COMMON NAME: Black Coral

SCIENTIFIC NAME: Antipatharia dichotoma

AVERAGE SIZE: Trees vary from a few feet across to 15 ft.

FAMILY: Coral - Pocillopora

DIET: Nutrients provided by plankton.

DEPTH FOUND: 15-50ft.

HABITAT: Black coral in Hawaii is rarely seen by scuba divers due to the fact that it grows best at depths past 100 feet. Black coral has been observed growing in as shallow as 35 ft., but most of the shallower Black coral has been harvested for jewelry. Black coral is actually reddish in color while it's alive, turning black once removed from the water. Found most often on deep slopes exposed to currents. If you find Black coral look for a Longnose hawkfish and check your depth gauge.

* * * * *

COMMON NAME: Cauliflower Coral

SCIENTIFIC NAME: Pocillopora meandrina

AVERAGE SIZE: 12-15in. across.

FAMILY: Coral - Pocillopora

DIET: Nutrients provided by sunlight and algae.

DEPTH FOUND: surge zone - 70ft.

HABITAT: Prefers shallow surge areas. Tends to be the first coral to colonize on new lava flow areas. This species provides homes and protection for many small fish and invertebrates. *Look for the Arc-eye Hawkfish.*

Antler
Coral

Black
Coral

Cauliflower
Coral

COMMON NAME: Finger Coral
SCIENTIFIC NAME: Porites compressa
AVERAGE SIZE: 4-6in.
FAMILY: Coral - Pocillopora
DIET: Nutrients provided by sunlight and algae.
DEPTH FOUND: 35-70ft.
HABITAT: Found on the leeward coast of the islands. Likes to inhabit deep slopes and calm clear bays. This is the second most common coral found in Hawaii. Finger coral grows rapidly in calm environments and will overgrow other coral at times. Finger coral provides homes to all kinds of small fish. Such as the Flame Anglefish.

COMMON NAME: Lobe Coral
SCIENTIFIC NAME: Porites lobata
AVERAGE SIZE: Variable.
FAMILY: Coral - Pocillopora
DIET: Nutrients provided by sunlight and algae.
DEPTH FOUND: surge zone - 50ft.
HABITAT: Found in shallow water. This is the most common form of coral found in the Hawaiian islands. Can form into large mounds. A favorite home for tube worms.

COMMON NAME: Orange Tube Coral
SCIENTIFIC NAME: Tubastraea coccinea
AVERAGE SIZE: 1 in.
FAMILY: Coral - Pocillopora
DIET: Nutrients provided by plankton.
DEPTH FOUND: 15-50ft.
HABITAT: This is the most colorful of all the corals in Hawaii. Grows most often on the ceiling of caverns and steep walls. This coral lacks the algae that is associated with other corals, thus getting all its nutrients from feeding on plankton in the currents.

Finger
Coral

Lobe
Coral

Orange Tube
Coral

COMMON NAME: Plate Coral

SCIENTIFIC NAME: Porites (synaraea) rus

AVERAGE SIZE: Variable.

FAMILY: Coral - Pocillopora

DIET: Nutrients provided by sunlight and algae.

DEPTH FOUND: 60-100+ft.

HABITAT: Usually forms large beds in deep calm clear bays on the leeward side of the islands. The Sergeant Major fish likes to lay its eggs on the dead plate coral.

COMMON NAME: Mushroom or Razor Coral

SCIENTIFIC NAME: Fungia scutaria

AVERAGE SIZE: 3-5in.

FAMILY: Coral - Pocillopora

DIET: Nutrients provided through algae and sunlight.

DEPTH FOUND: 15-50ft.

HABITAT: This is an unattached coral. Found laying on the bottom loose. Top side is sharp with underside being smoother. Immature mushroom corals are attached until they're about 1 inch in size.

* * * * *

COMMON NAME: Wire Coral

SCIENTIFIC NAME: Cirrhipathes anguina

AVERAGE SIZE: 4ft.

FAMILY: Coral - Pocillopora

DIET: Nutrients are provided by plankton.

DEPTH FOUND: 35-100+ft.

HABITAT: Wire coral is a common Hawaiian coral. It varies in color from green to brown. If you look closely you might see the shrimp, or more likely the gobies that live their entire life on an individual Wire coral. This coral is found in areas of currents either growing off walls or straight up from the reef on deep slopes.

Plate
Coral

Razor
Coral

Wire
Coral

FISH FEEDING?

For the most part I don't advocate feeding the fish. This is due to the fact that it really changes their behavior, and the social structure of the reef. It is also a good way to get bit by eels or other aggressive fish. If you choose to ignore my warning then don't blame the fish that bites you, they're just looking for food and don't understand the rules.

BUTTERFLYFISH FACTS

Some of the most colorful fish you'll find on the reef are in the Butterflyfish family. They are usually seen in pairs and busily feeding by day. These fish can be seen in shallow bays to well past 200 ft. In Hawaii we have about 22 species with 3 being endemic (found only in Hawaii). For most of the Butterflyfish, feeding occurs during the daytime hours. Their diet varies from plankton to small invertebrates. At night Butterfly fish (with one exception *see Raccoon Butterflyfish*), rest in crevices around the coral in a dormant state . Their color pattern loses its daytime brilliance and takes on a more somber colorations. For defensive purposes most Butterflyfish have a dark band through the eye, and an eye spot near the tail to confuse their predators, such as the Moray Eel. Butterflyfish are believed to mate for years and maybe even life. The reproduction process occurs with the release of eggs that are fertilized at the same time and allowed to be carried off into the current. The eggs will hatch, go through a larval stage, with the survivors settling in to a niche on the reef. Juveniles often seek the protection of shallow bays. As they mature they will pair up and inhabit deeper seaward reefs. Most Butterflyfish tend to roam in the same territory during their life cycle.

COMMON NAME: Tinkers Butterflyfish

SCIENTIFIC NAME: Chaetodon tinkeri

AVERAGE SIZE: 4-6 in.

FAMILY: Butterflyfish - Chaetodontidae

DIET: Planktonic invertebrates.

DEPTH FOUND: 70-200+ft.

HABITAT and BEHAVIOR: This is a rare fish to spot in water shallower than 100 plus feet due to their attraction to deep water. Generally found in pairs, once encountered, Tinkers are usually curious and quite approachable. They are usually found along current swept dropoffs.

DISTRIBUTION: Once believed to be endemic to Hawaii. Tinkers have been found in waters off the Marshall Islands.

Tinkers
Butterflyfish

Tinkers
Butterflyfish

COMMON NAME: Blacklip or Klein's Butterflyfish
SCIENTIFIC NAME: Chaetodon kleinii
AVERAGE SIZE: 4in.
FAMILY: Butterflyfish - Chaetodontidae
DIET: Feeds mainly on zooplankton.
DEPTH FOUND: 60-100+ft.
HABITAT and BEHAVIOR: This is a common fish to spot below 60 ft. Generally found singularly or in pairs. This fish is easily approached by the quiet diver.
DISTRIBUTION: Found throughout the Indo Pacific.

COMMON NAME: Bluestripe Butterflyfish
SCIENTIFIC NAME: Chaetodon fremblii
AVERAGE SIZE: 4-6in.
FAMILY: Butterflyfish - Chaetodontidae
DIET: Small invertebrates.
DEPTH FOUND: 10-90ft.
HABITAT and BEHAVIOR: This is a common fish to spot on the reef in Hawaii. Bluestripes are often found singularly, and in pairs, (as with most Butterflyfish). This fish is easily approached by the courteous snorkeler or diver.
DISTRIBUTION: Endemic to Hawaii.

COMMON NAME: Lined Butterflyfish
SCIENTIFIC NAME: Chaetodon lineolatus
AVERAGE SIZE: 10-12in. (largest in the family).
FAMILY: Butterflyfish - Chaetodontidae
DIET: Coral polyps, small invertebrates and algae.
DEPTH FOUND: 10-100+ft.
HABITAT and BEHAVIOR: Lined Butterflyfish can be found in about any depth inside lagoons and on outer reefs. This fish seems to have a large grazing territory. Lined Butterflyfish are very skittish and extremely difficult to approach. Uncommon in Hawaii.
DISTRIBUTION: From the Red Sea to the Central and Western Pacific.

Blacklip Butterflyfish

Kikakapu

Bluestripe Butterflyfish

Kikakapu

Lined Butterflyfish

Kikakapu

COMMON NAME: Fourspot Butterflyfish

SCIENTIFIC NAME: Chaetodon quadrimaculatus

AVERAGE SIZE: 4-6in.

FAMILY: Butterflyfish - Chaetodontidae

DIET: Coral polyps.

DEPTH FOUND: 10-50ft.

HABITAT and BEHAVIOR: Found mainly on outer reefs. Usually paired and generally easy to approach.

DISTRIBUTION: Hawaii and throughout Central Polynesia to southern Japan.

✳ ✳ ✳ ✳ ✳

COMMON NAME: Long-nosed Butterflyfish

SCIENTIFIC NAME: Forcipiger longirostris

AVERAGE SIZE: 5-7in.

FAMILY: Butterflyfish - Chaetodontidae

DIET: Feeds on small invertebrates, fish eggs and tube worms.

DEPTH FOUND: 10-100+ft.

HABITAT AND BEHAVIOR: Often mistaken for its close relative the Forceps fish because of their shape. The easiest way to distinguish between the two is to take note of the mouth, the Forceps has a split at the opening while the Long-nose has a longer snout with no visible split. One other distinctive difference is the blackish spots on the chest of only the Long-nose. Both of these fish use their long nose to reach into crevices or coral to reach their prey. In Hawaiian waters, this species can be found in two color phases; all black or the more common yellow with white. Found most often on seaward reefs. Not as common in lagoons and bays. This fish tends to favor water 60ft and deeper. Usually easy to approach.

DISTRIBUTION: From The Red Sea to Mexico and throughout the Central and Western Pacific.

✳ ✳ ✳ ✳ ✳

COMMON NAME: Forceps Butterflyfish

SCIENTIFIC NAME: Forcipiger flavissimus

AVERAGE SIZE: 4-6in.

FAMILY: Butterflyfish - Chaetodontidae

DIET: Small invertebrates, fish eggs, and the tubed feet of sea urchins.

DEPTH FOUND: 10-100+ft.

HABITAT and BEHAVIOR: Found most often on seaward reefs. Not as common in lagoons and bays. This fish is usually easy to approach. *SEE Long-nose Butterflyfish*

DISTRIBUTION: From The Red Sea to Mexico and throughout the Central and Western Pacific.

Fourspot
Butterflyfish

Lau-Hau

Long-nose
Butterflyfish

Lau-wiliwili-
nukunuku-'oi'oi

Forceps
Butterflyfish

Lau-wiliwili-
nukunuku-'oi'oi

COMMON NAME: Milletseed or Lemon Butterflyfish
SCIENTIFIC NAME: Chaetodon miliaris
AVERAGE SIZE: 4in.
FAMILY: Butterflyfish - Chaetodontidae
DIET: Zooplankton.
DEPTH FOUND: 10-90ft.
HABITAT and BEHAVIOR: This is one of the most common fish on the reef in Hawaii. This species often schools up off the reef, feeding in the current. Lemon Butterflyfish are generally easily approached by the non-threatening snorkeler or diver.
DISTRIBUTION: Endemic to Hawaii.

✳ ✳ ✳ ✳ ✳

COMMON NAME: Multiband or Pebbled Butterflyfish
SCIENTIFIC NAME: Chaetodon multicinctus
AVERAGE SIZE: 4in.
FAMILY: Butterflyfish - Chaetodontidae
DIET: Coral polyps.
DEPTH FOUND: 10-90ft.
HABITAT and BEHAVIOR: Most often seen in pairs or large schools. This is a common fish to spot on the reef in Hawaii. This fish is easily approached by the non-threatening snorkeler or diver.
DISTRIBUTION: Endemic to Hawaii.

✳ ✳ ✳ ✳ ✳

COMMON NAME: Ornate Butterflyfish
SCIENTIFIC NAME: Chaetodon ornatissimus
AVERAGE SIZE: 6-8in.
FAMILY: Butterflyfish - Chaetodontidae
DIET: Coral polyp tissue particularly damaged areas.
DEPTH FOUND: 10-90ft.
HABITAT and BEHAVIOR: As juveniles, Ornates live singularly amongst coral branches. Upon reaching adulthood they pair up and become territorial. Seen most often on the outer reefs where they are easily observed during the day.
DISTRIBUTION: Large distribution throughout the Central and Western Pacific.

Lemon
Butterflyfish

Lau-wili wili

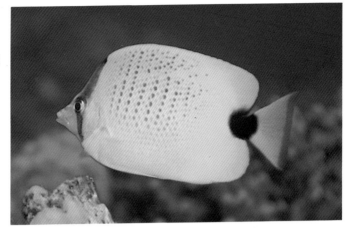

Pebbled
Butterflyfish

Kikakapu

Ornate
Butterflyfish

Kikakapu

COMMON NAME: Oval or Redfin Butterflyfish
SCIENTIFIC NAME: Chaetodon trifasciatus
AVERAGE SIZE: 4-6in.
FAMILY: Butterflyfish - Chaetodontidae
DIET: Almost exclusively on coral polyps.
DEPTH FOUND: 10-60ft.
HABITAT and BEHAVIOR: Found inhabiting coral lagoons and other protected seaward reefs. Possessing a strong mating bond, Ovals are shy to the approach of divers and snorkelers.
DISTRIBUTION: From East Africa to the Central and Western Pacific.

COMMON NAME: Pyramid Butterflyfish
SCIENTIFIC NAME: Hemitaurichthys polylepis
AVERAGE SIZE: 5in.
FAMILY: Butterflyfish - Chaetodontidae
DIET: Zooplankton.
DEPTH FOUND: 20-120+ft.
HABITAT and BEHAVIOR: Found schooling up off the reef in the water column, feeding. Pyramids tend to congregate near current swept dropoffs, which supports their feeding habits. This fish is generally easily approached.
DISTRIBUTION: Large distribution throughout the Central and Western Pacific.

COMMON NAME: Pennant or Banner Butterflyfish
SCIENTIFIC NAME: Heniochus diphreutes
AVERAGE SIZE: 5-7in.
FAMILY: Butterflyfish - Chaetodontidae
DIET: Zooplankton.
DEPTH FOUND: 50-100+ft.
HABITAT and BEHAVIOR: Found in schools feeding in the water column, Pennetfish prefer water dephts of 70+ feet. Pennantfish look similar to the Moorish Idol but with a reverse color pattern. This fish is generally easy to approach.
DISTRIBUTION: Found from the shores of the Red Sea, to Australia, Hawaii and the south coast of Africa.

Oval
Butterflyfish

Kapuhili

Pyramid
Butterflyfish

Pennant
Butterflyfish

COMMON NAME: Raccoon Butterflyfish

SCIENTIFIC NAME: Chaetodon lunula

AVERAGE SIZE: 5-7in.

FAMILY: Butterflyfish - Chaetodontidae

DIET: Nudibranchs, small invertebrates, tube worm tentacles and occasionally, coral polyps and algae.

DEPTH FOUND: 10-90ft.

HABITAT and BEHAVIOR: Raccoons are the only nocturnal feeders in the Butterflyfish family. They are easily observed during the day in a variety of reef locations. Raccoons are found in schools and in pairs, (as with most butterflyfish). This fish is shy upon approach.

DISTRIBUTION: Large distribution from Hawaii to East Africa.

✳   ✳   ✳   ✳   ✳

COMMON NAME: Reticulated Butterflyfish

SCIENTIFIC NAME: Chaetodon reticulatus

AVERAGE SIZE: 4-6 in.

FAMILY: Butterflyfish - Chaetodontidae

DIET: Coral polyps.

DEPTH FOUND: 10-90ft.

HABITAT and BEHAVIOR: This is an uncommon fish to spot on the reef. Reticulates are often found in pairs, (as with most butterflyfish), they busily work their way around the reef feeding on coral polyps. Generally shy upon approach.

DISTRIBUTION: Found in areas between Hawaii and the Philippines.

✳   ✳   ✳   ✳   ✳

COMMON NAME: Saddleback Butterflyfish

SCIENTIFIC NAME: Chaetodon ephippium

AVERAGE SIZE: 6-9in.

FAMILY: Butterflyfish - Chaetodontidae

DIET: Coral polyps, sponges, small invertebrates, fish eggs, and algae.

DEPTH FOUND: 10-90ft.

HABITAT and BEHAVIOR: This is an uncommon fish to spot on the reef. Saddlebacks are often found in pairs, (as with most butterflyfish), or in small schools. Saddlebacks are usually skittish when approached.

DISTRIBUTION: Found in areas between Hawaii and the Philippines and throughout Micronesia.

Raccoon
Butterflyfish

Kikakapu

Reticulated
Butterflyfish

Saddleback
Butterflyfish

COMMON NAME: Teardrop Butterflyfish
SCIENTIFIC NAME: Chaetodon unimaculatus
AVERAGE SIZE: 5-7in.
FAMILY: Butterflyfish - Chaetodontidae
DIET: Coral polyps (hard and soft corals), small crustaceans and algae.
DEPTH FOUND: 20-100ft.
HABITAT and BEHAVIOR: Uncommon on most Hawaiian reefs. Teardrops tend to be shy with divers and snorkelers. The adults pair up and are territorial. Not as common in shallow lagoons as some of the other Butterflyfish. Teardrops are most often seen grazing the seaward reef during the day feeding on coral polyps.
DISTRIBUTION: Large distribution throughout the Central and Western Pacific.

COMMON NAME: Thompson's Butterflyfish
SCIENTIFIC NAME: Hemitaurichthys thompsoni
AVERAGE SIZE: 5-7in.
FAMILY: Butterflyfish - Chaetodontidae
DIET: Zooplankton
DEPTH FOUND: 50-100+ft.
HABITAT and BEHAVIOR: Found schooling over the reef in the water column feeding, often in large schools. Thompson's are the only species in the Butterflyfish family which are uniformly dark gray to black. This fish is generally easy to approach.
DISTRIBUTION: Very localized in distribution found in the Marianas, Samoa, Hawaii, and the Tuamotu Islands.

✳ ✳ ✳ ✳ ✳

COMMON NAME: Threadfin Butterflyfish
SCIENTIFIC NAME: Chaetodon auriga
AVERAGE SIZE: 5-7in.
FAMILY: Butterflyfish - Chaetodontidae
DIET: Coral Polyps, polychaetes, and algae
DEPTH FOUND: 10-100ft.
HABITAT and BEHAVIOR: Found mainly on outer reefs, usually paired. Threadfins stay close to their home territory. These fish are usually shy upon approach.
DISTRIBUTION: From the Red Seas to the Central and Western Pacific.

Teardrop
Butterflyfish

Lau-Hau

Thompson's
Butterflyfish

Threadfin
Butterflyfish

Kikakapu

WRASSE FACTS

The Wrasse family is a very diverse category of fish. This family contains a group that have brilliantly complex color patterns that can change with age or sex. Hawaiian wrasses found on the reef vary in size from 2 to 15in.

Wrasses are generally carnivorous, they feed on invertebrates or smaller fishes. There are some that feed on plankton while others are cleaners that feed on parasites from other fish, such as the Cleaner Wrasse. Their predominate colors are the greens, blues, and yellows. Most Wrasses have noticeable front teeth that are used to eat invertebrates.

Wrasses forage for food during the daytime and become inactive at night. Most sleep under the sand.

The Wrasse family has one of the most interesting and complex social structures. As juveniles, male and female wrasses usually look alike. As they mature some of the females change sex and evolve to become supermales who are the largest and most brilliantly colored of the species. This is determined by the type of mating system the species of wrasses engages in.

There are two recognized mating systems for Wrasses. The first one, "*Leks*", is where several males congregate at a temporary mating site and defend a small territory while mating with several females.

The second method involves the *Harem system.* In the Harem System, one male maintains his own harem of females which he mates exclusively with. In either case the mating interaction is very competitive amongst the males.

The female has the ability to change sex. Sex changes are influenced by the female wrasses' social environment and most often occurs to replace the male who recently died, thus taking over the harem. This transition takes place fairly rapidly so that another male from an associated reef doesn't take control of the harem. The initial males cannot change sexes.

COMMON NAME: Bird Wrasse

SCIENTIFIC NAME: Gomphosus varius

AVERAGE SIZE: 6-8in.

FAMILY: Wrasse - Labridae

DIET: Feeds on crustaceans, (crabs and shrimp) brittle stars, and mollusks.

DEPTH FOUND: 15-100ft.

HABITAT and BEHAVIOR: Bird Wrasses are commonly found close to shore in Hawaii. These fish use their long snout to probe into crevices and coral for food. Seen singularly and in groups of 5-7. This is an active swimming wrasse, thus making it difficult to get close to.

DISTRIBUTION: Found throughout the Indo Pacific.

Male Bird
Wrasse

Aki-Lolo

Female Bird
Wrasse

Aki-Lolo

COMMON NAME: Blacktail Wrasse
SCIENTIFIC NAME: Thalassoma ballieui
AVERAGE SIZE: 10-12in.
FAMILY: Wrasse - Labridae
DIET: Feeds on crabs, and a variety of other small invertebrates.
DEPTH FOUND: 20-80ft.
HABITAT and BEHAVIOR: Found actively swimming above the reef in search of food. Easily approached. This species goes through very little color changes as it matures.
DISTRIBUTION: Endemic to Hawaii.

COMMON NAME: Ornate Wrasse
SCIENTIFIC NAME: Halichoeres ornatissimus
AVERAGE SIZE: 4-6in.
FAMILY: Wrasse - Labridae
DIET: Feeds on small crustaceans and mollusks.
DEPTH FOUND: 5-70ft.
HABITAT and BEHAVIOR: Common fish found actively swimming close to the bottom. This species is shy and difficult to approach.
DISTRIBUTION: Found from Hawaii to the Central Pacific.

COMMON NAME: Belted Wrasse
SCIENTIFIC NAME: Stethojulis balteata
AVERAGE SIZE: 3-5in.
FAMILY: Wrasse - Labridae
DIET: Various small crustaceans, small polychaete, and peanut worms.
DEPTH FOUND: 5-50ft.
HABITAT and BEHAVIOR: Belted wrasses are very active shoreline fish. Commonly found close to or in the surge zone. Due to the fact that this species is so active it is difficult to approach, or should I say catch up with.
DISTRIBUTION: Endemic to Hawaii.

**Blacktail
Wrasse**

Hinalea Luahine

**Ornate
Wrasse**

Hilu

**Belted
Wrasse**

Omaka

COMMON NAME: Christmas Wrasse
SCIENTIFIC NAME: Thalassoma trilobatum
AVERAGE SIZE: 7-10in.
FAMILY: Wrasse - Labridae
DIET: Feeds on small invertebrates and mollusks.
DEPTH FOUND: 5-40ft.
HABITAT and BEHAVIOR: The Christmas wrasse is commonly found in very shallow water to usually no deeper then 40ft. This is a very active swimming wrasse thus making it difficult to get close to. Christmas wrasses are common in shallow bays and surge sweeped coastlines.
DISTRIBUTION: Found from East Africa, throughout Micronesia and Hawaii.

✳ ✳ ✳ ✳ ✳

COMMON NAME: Eightline Wrasse
SCIENTIFIC NAME: Pseudocheilinus octotaenia
AVERAGE SIZE: 3-5in.
FAMILY: Wrasse - Labridae
DIET: Feeds on small crustaceans and mollusks.
DEPTH FOUND: 5-100+ft.
HABITAT and BEHAVIOR: Common fish found living close to the bottom. If you stay in one spot for a few minutes this fish will often get curious and approach within a few feet of you.
DISTRIBUTION: Found throughout the Indo Pacific.

✳ ✳ ✳ ✳ ✳

COMMON NAME: Hawaiian Cleaner Wrasse
SCIENTIFIC NAME: Labroides phthirophagus
AVERAGE SIZE: 2-3in.
FAMILY: Wrasse - Labridae
DIET: This fish establishes a cleaning station on the reef where resident fish come to have parasites removed by the Cleaner Wrasse. The Cleaner Wrasse is also known to feed on mucous and some of the host's scales.
DEPTH FOUND: 5-100+ft.
HABITAT and BEHAVIOR: Cleaner wrasses move about with a darting motion. When a another fish swims into a cleaning station the wrasse will begin to peck and remove the parasites on the host fish. The Cleaner Wrasse is also responsible for dental care and will often go into the mouth of larger fishes and come out the gills or visa versa. Cleaner Wrasses don't bury themselves in the sand at night like most wrasses, instead the they become inactive and form a mucus cocoon similar to the Parrot Fish.
DISTRIBUTION: Endemic to Hawaii.

Christmas
Wrasse

Awela

Eightline
Wrasse

Hawaiian
Cleaner
Wrasse

COMMON NAME: Pacific Hogfish
SCIENTIFIC NAME: Bodianus bilunulatus
AVERAGE SIZE: 15-20in.
FAMILY: Wrasse - Labridae
DIET: Feeds on mollusks, crabs, brittle stars and small fish.
DEPTH FOUND: 25-100ft.
HABITAT and BEHAVIOR: Hogfish swim near the bottom foraging for food. They will often follow close to divers watching for the diver to disrupt the bottom that exposes food for the Hogfish. Commonly found on seaward reefs.
DISTRIBUTION: From Hawaii and throughout the Central and Western Pacific to the Indian Ocean.

✳ ✳ ✳ ✳ ✳

COMMON NAME: Rockmover
SCIENTIFIC NAME: Novaculichthys taeniourus
AVERAGE SIZE: 10-12in.
FAMILY: Wrasse - Labridae
DIET: Small invertebrates, brittle stars, sea urchins and Polychaete
DEPTH FOUND: 20-70ft.
HABITAT and BEHAVIOR: The Rockmover likes areas with sand and loose coral so that they can turn over rocks searching for food. This is one of the most active fish on the reef. *The juvenile is known as Dragon Wrasse.*
DISTRIBUTION: From The Red Sea to Panama and throughout the Central and Western Pacific.

✳ ✳ ✳ ✳ ✳

COMMON NAME: Dragon Wrasse
SCIENTIFIC NAME: Novaculichthys taeniourus
AVERAGE SIZE: 2-3in.
FAMILY: Wrasse - Labridae
DIET: Small invertebrates, brittle stars, sea urchins and Polychaete
DEPTH FOUND: 20-70ft.
HABITAT and BEHAVIOR: This is a juvenile Rockmover. As juveniles these fish live in areas of light surge and mimic a drifting piece of algae. The juvenile will go through some drastic color and pattern changes before maturity. *SEE Rockmover*
DISTRIBUTION: From The Red Sea to Panama and throughout the Central and Western Pacific.

Pacific
Hogfish
Wrasse

A'awa

Rockmover
Wrasse

Dragon
Wrasse

COMMON NAME: Razorfish
SCIENTIFIC NAME: Xyrichtys pavo
AVERAGE SIZE: 10-12in.
FAMILY: Wrasse - Labridae
DIET: Feeds on crabs and a variety of small invertebrates.
DEPTH FOUND: 50-100ft.
HABITAT and BEHAVIOR: To find this fish, you will need to look in large sandy areas where they live. Razorfish will dive into the sand and burrow away from any potential danger. Juveniles (seen here) have a long banner like fin near the top of their head that shortens with maturity.
DISTRIBUTION: Found throughout the Indo Pacific.

COMMON NAME: Ringtail Wrasse
SCIENTIFIC NAME: Cheilinus unifasciatus
AVERAGE SIZE: 10-12in.
FAMILY: Wrasse - Labridae
DIET: Feeds on small fish, crabs,and a variety of sea urchins.
DEPTH FOUND: 30-100+ft.
HABITAT and BEHAVIOR: Common fish found above the reef stalking small fish or crabs. This species is capable of rapid color changes. It's not recommended for consumption due to possible ciguatera poisoning.
DISTRIBUTION: Found throughout the Central and Western Pacific.

COMMON NAME: Psychedelic Wrasse
SCIENTIFIC NAME: Anampses chrysocephalus
AVERAGE SIZE: 5-7in.
FAMILY: Wrasse - Labridae
DIET: Feeds on small invertebrates.
DEPTH FOUND: 50+ft.
HABITAT and BEHAVIOR: This is a rarely observed wrasse on most Hawaiian reefs. Psychedelics move quickly, and close to the bottom searching for food. Very shy fish, difficult to approach.
DISTRIBUTION: Endemic to Hawaii.

Razorfish
Wrasse

Ringtail
Wrasse

Psychodelic
Wrasse

COMMON NAME: Saddle Wrasse
SCIENTIFIC NAME: Thalassoma duperrey
AVERAGE SIZE: 7-10in.
FAMILY: Wrasse - Labridae
DIET: Feeds on crabs, and a variety of small invertebrates.
DEPTH FOUND: 10-100ft.
HABITAT and BEHAVIOR: These fish are the most common of all the reef fish found in Hawaii. Found in areas with rubble bottoms which favors their feeding habits, this species has been observed periodically cleaning larger fish. Saddlebacks are easy to approach. Often they will approach you.
DISTRIBUTION: Endemic to Hawaii.

COMMON NAME: Shortnose Wrasse
SCIENTIFIC NAME: Macropharyngodon geoffroy
AVERAGE SIZE: 4-6in.
FAMILY: Wrasse - Labridae
DIET: Feeds on mollusks.
DEPTH FOUND: 20-100ft.
HABITAT and BEHAVIOR: The Shortnose Wrasse is commonly found in areas with mixed sand and rubble. Common to find on outer reef areas. Active swimming wrasse, thus making it difficult to get close to. Males have more orange coloration the on head and nose.
DISTRIBUTION: Endemic to Hawaii.

Saddle
Wrasse

Hinalea
Lau-Wili

Female
Shortnose
Wrasse

Male
Shortnose
Wrasse

COMMON NAME: Sunset Wrasse
SCIENTIFIC NAME: Thalassoma lutescens
AVERAGE SIZE: 6-8in.
FAMILY: Wrasse - Labridae
DIET: Feeds on crabs, and a variety of small invertebrates.
DEPTH FOUND: 10-100ft.
HABITAT and BEHAVIOR: This species behavior is almost identical as the Saddle Wrasse. Periodically seen schooling with the Saddle Wrasse. Commonly found actively swimming on the open reef. Easily approached.
DISTRIBUTION: Found throughout the Indo-Pacific.

* * * * *

COMMON NAME: Yellowtail Coris
SCIENTIFIC NAME: Coris gaimard
AVERAGE SIZE: 12-15in.
FAMILY: Wrasse - Labridae
DIET: Feeds mainly on crabs, mollusks and hermit crabs.
DEPTH FOUND: 25-100ft.
HABITAT and BEHAVIOR: These fish are commonly found in areas with rubble bottoms which favors their feeding habits. Generally common and easy to approach.
DISTRIBUTION: From Hawaii and throughout the Central and Western Pacific.

* * * * *

COMMON NAME: Juvenile Yellowtail Coris
SCIENTIFIC NAME: Coris gaimard
AVERAGE SIZE: to 3in.
FAMILY: Wrasse - Labridae
DIET: Feeds mainly on crabs, mollusks and hermit crabs.
DEPTH FOUND: 25-100ft.
HABITAT and BEHAVIOR: These fish are commonly found in areas with rubble bottoms which favors their feeding habits. These fish are common and easy to approach.
DISTRIBUTION: From Hawaii and throughout the Central and Western Pacific.

Sunset
Wrasse

Yellowtail
Wrasse

Hinalea
'Aki-Lolo

Juvenile
Yellowtail
Wrasse

COMMON NAME: Surge Wrasse

SCIENTIFIC NAME: Thalassoma purpureum

AVERAGE SIZE: 8-10in.

FAMILY: Wrasse - Labridae

DIET: Feeds on crabs, and a variety of small invertebrates.

DEPTH FOUND: 5-30ft.

HABITAT and BEHAVIOR: Found almost exclusively in the surge zone. This is a very active swimmer with a variable diet. Difficult to get close to due to its constant motion. If pursued these fish will take refuge in very shallow turbulent water.

DISTRIBUTION: Found throughout the Indo-Pacific.

COMMON NAME: Smalltail Wrasse

SCIENTIFIC NAME: Pseudojuloides cerasinus

AVERAGE SIZE: 3-4in.

FAMILY: Wrasse - Labridae

DIET: Feeds on mollusks.

DEPTH FOUND: 20-100ft.

HABITAT and BEHAVIOR: Found swimming very close to the bottom in depths that exceed 60ft. This fish is shy and prefers rubble bottoms. The best approach technique is passive, since Smalltails are cautious, but curious, and often will approach a motionless diver. Females are bright orange.

DISTRIBUTION: Found throughout the Indo Pacific.

**Surge
Wrasse**

Hou

**Smalltail
Wrasse**

SURGEON FISH FACTS

The Surgeonfish family, (also known as the Tang family), get their name for the scalpel like spines located on each side of the body near the base of their tail. Some of these fish have rigid spines while others can fold the spine almost flush against the body.

Reproduction is accomplished by the release of the eggs into the current, followed by fertilization by the male. Due to a long larvae period, this species is widespread.

Surgeonfish are one of the most conservatively colored of the tropicals, the Yellow tang being the only exception. You will find most surgeonfish are algae feeders and found in shallow waters. They also can be difficult to approach. At night Surgeonfish hide in the crevices of the reef. hoping to avoid being fed upon by the moray eel.

COMMON NAME: Bluespine Unicornfish

SCIENTIFIC NAME: Naso unicornis

AVERAGE SIZE: 15-20in.

FAMILY: Surgeonfish - Acanthuridae

DIET: Feeds on leafy brown algae.

DEPTH FOUND: 10-100+ft.

HABITAT and BEHAVIOR: Often found in shallow surging water. But will also inhabit deeper exposed seaward reefs. Easily identified by its horn and blue spines near the tail. This species is very shy upon approach generally keeping its distance.

DISTRIBUTION: From the Red Sea, the coast of Africa and throughout the Pacific to Hawaii.

* * * * *

COMMON NAME: Chevron Tang

SCIENTIFIC NAME: Ctenochaetus hawaiiensis

AVERAGE SIZE: 8-10in.

FAMILY: Surgeonfish - Acanthuridae

DIET: Feeds on dietrus.

DEPTH FOUND: Surface - 100+ft.

HABITAT and BEHAVIOR: This is a common species in Hawaii that is usually observed in coral rich shallow lagoons and bays. As they mature their colors begin to fade to almost totally black. Adults are very common.

DISTRIBUTION: This is a very common species in Hawaii, but rare in other parts of the Central Pacific.

**Bluespine
Surgeonfish**

Kala

**Chevron Tang
Surgeonfish**

COMMON NAME: Eye striped Surgeonfish
SCIENTIFIC NAME: Acanthurus dussumieri
AVERAGE SIZE: 18in.
FAMILY: Surgeonfish - Acanthuridae
DIET: Feeds near the surface on fine green and bluegreen algae. Eye stripes will also eat algae from hard surfaces, such as rock or coral.
DEPTH FOUND: 30-100+ft.
HABITAT and BEHAVIOR: This species is a daytime feeder that is usually found in water greater than 30ft. Most often found on the open seaward reef. Hides in holes at night for protection.
DISTRIBUTION: Found in the Indo Pacific, but only in the Hawaiian part of the Central Pacific.

COMMON NAME: Goldring Surgeonfish
SCIENTIFIC NAME: Ctenochaetus strigosus
AVERAGE SIZE: 5-7in.
FAMILY: Surgeonfish - Acanthuridae
DIET: Feeds on dietrus
DEPTH FOUND: Surface - 100+ft.
HABITAT and BEHAVIOR: This is a common species in Hawaii that is usually observed in coral rich shallow lagoons and bays. Will school in the hundreds at times.
DISTRIBUTION: Common species in Hawaii, but rare in other parts of the Central Pacific. Also found in the Indian Ocean and the East Coast of Africa.

COMMON NAME: Convict Tang
SCIENTIFIC NAME: Acanthurus sandvicensis
AVERAGE SIZE: 4-5in.
FAMILY: Surgeonfish - Acanthuridae
DIET: Feeds on several different types of filamentous algae.
DEPTH FOUND: surface - 100+ft.
HABITAT and BEHAVIOR: This species is a subspecies of the triostegus that is found in other parts of the Pacific. The Hawaiian Convict Tang is probably the most abundant of the surgeonfish found on the reef, often seen grazing the reef in large schools. This allows the fish to overwhelm any territorial fish such as a Damselfish when grazing.
DISTRIBUTION: This subspecies is endemic to Hawaii.

Eye striped
Surgeonfish

Palani

Goldring
Surgeonfish

Kole

Convict Tang
Surgeonfish

Manini

COMMON NAME: Orange Band Surgeonfish
SCIENTIFIC NAME: Acanthurus olivaceus
AVERAGE SIZE: 12in.
FAMILY: Surgeonfish - Acanthuridae
DIET: Feeds on the surface film of detritus, diatoms and filamentous algae.
DEPTH FOUND: 30-100ft.
HABITAT and BEHAVIOR: This species goes through some dramatic color changes as it matures. Juveniles are yellow and then gradually turn grayish brown with the orange stripe behind the eye. Most often observed over sandy bottoms and rubble areas. This is a common fish that is easily to approached.
DISTRIBUTION: From Hawaii to throughout the Central Pacific.

COMMON NAME: Orange Spine Unicornfish
SCIENTIFIC NAME: Naso lituratus
AVERAGE SIZE: 15-18in.
FAMILY: Surgeonfish - Acanthuridae
DIET: Feeds on leafy brown algae.
DEPTH FOUND: 10-100+ft.
HABITAT and BEHAVIOR: The Orange Spine is a hornless unicornfish that is very common in Hawaii, found feeding amongst coral, rock, and rubble bottoms. Easy to approach.
DISTRIBUTION: From the Red Sea, the coast of Africa and throughout the Pacific to Hawaii.

Orange Band
Surgeonfish

Na'ena'e

Orange Spine
Surgeonfish

Umaumalei

COMMON NAME: Whitebar Surgeonfish
SCIENTIFIC NAME: Acanthurus leucopareius
AVERAGE SIZE: 7-9in.
FAMILY: Surgeonfish - Acanthuridae
DIET: Feeds on filamentous algae.
DEPTH FOUND: 5-30+ft.
HABITAT and BEHAVIOR: Often found in large schools in the surge zone grazing amongst the boulders. Whitebars are shy upon approach.
DISTRIBUTION: Found in only a few locations, such as: Hawaii, S. Japan, Marianas, New Caledonia and Easter Island.

COMMON NAME: Whitespotted Surgeonfish
SCIENTIFIC NAME: Acanthurus guttatus
AVERAGE SIZE: 9-11in.
FAMILY: Surgeonfish - Acanthuridae
DIET: Feeds on filamentous algae.
DEPTH FOUND: 5-30+ft.
HABITAT and BEHAVIOR: Often found in large schools in the surge zone. Grazes the reef feeding on algae using the shallow turbulent water as it primary protection against predators. The white spots may also provide some camouflage as they may simulate the swirling white bubbles of the surf action, thus confusing predators.
DISTRIBUTION: Found throughout the Indo Pacific.

* * * * *

COMMON NAME: Yellow Tang
SCIENTIFIC NAME: Zebrasoma flavescens
AVERAGE SIZE: 4-6in.
FAMILY: Surgeonfish - Acanthuridae
DIET: Feeds on filamentous algae
DEPTH FOUND: 15-100+ft.
HABITAT and BEHAVIOR: One of the most common fish on the reef. Often the first fish recognized by beginning snorkelers or divers. Yellow Tangs graze the reef throughout the daytime and find a niche to hide in during the night.
DISTRIBUTION: Found from Hawaii to the Indian Ocean.

Whitebar
Surgeonfish

Maikoiko

White-Spotted
Surgeonfish

'Api

Yellow Tang
Surgeonfish

Lau'i-pala

COMMON NAME: Achilles Tang

SCIENTIFIC NAME: Ancanthurus achilles

AVERAGE SIZE: 7-10in.

FAMILY: Surgeonfish - Acanthuridae

DIET: Feeds on filamentous and small fleshy algae.

DEPTH FOUND: 5-25ft.

HABITAT and BEHAVIOR: This species likes shallow surging water areas. Achilles tangs are quite territorial and show aggression toward other surgeonfish. This is a common fish, but since it enjoys shallow, surging water, it is difficult to approach unless the water is quite calm. Feeds throughout the daytime and finds a niche to hide in during the night. Juveniles lack the large orange spot.

DISTRIBUTION: From Hawaii to throughout the Central Pacific.

COMMON NAME: Sailfin Tang

SCIENTIFIC NAME: Zebrasoma veliferum

AVERAGE SIZE: 10-13in.

FAMILY: Surgeonfish - Acanthuridae

DIET: Feeds on filamentous algae.

DEPTH FOUND: 5-100+ft.

HABITAT and BEHAVIOR: Found in lagoons and seaward reefs, generally in the lower surge zone. This is a common shallow water species in Hawaii. Sailfins are difficult to closely approach.

DISTRIBUTION: Found throughout the Indo Pacific.

Achilles Tang
Surgeonfish

Paku-iku'i

Sailfin Tang
Surgeonfish

Mane'one'o

BLENNY FACTS

Blennies are small elongated fish that live in water as shallow as the tide pools. Generally Blennies are found on the bottom where some of them feed on coral polyps and algae, while others are carnivorous. These are common fish, but due to their size, you have to look closely in order to find them.

COMMON NAME: Leopard or Shortbodied Blenny

SCIENTIFIC NAME: Exalias brevis

AVERAGE SIZE: 4-6in.

FAMILY: Blenny - Blenniidae

DIET: Feeds on coral polyps.

DEPTH FOUND: 10-25ft.

HABITAT and BEHAVIOR: Leopard blennies are very shy fish that hide deep in the coral. The males are the brightly colored of the species and tend to be territorial. When mating, the males will provide many nests for females to lay eggs in. Females will move between nests and deposit eggs in more than one. This species is uncommon in Hawaii.

DISTRIBUTION: From the Red Sea and throughout the Pacific to Hawaii.

COMMON NAME: Sabertooth or Ewa Blenny

SCIENTIFIC NAME: Plagiotremus ewaensis

AVERAGE SIZE: 3-4in.

FAMILY: Blenny - Blenniidae

DIET: Feeds on small fish scales, epidermal tissue, and mucus.

DEPTH FOUND: 20-100+ft.

HABITAT and BEHAVIOR: This fish is nicknamed the "impostor". Sabertooths make their living in a dangerous but challenging way. They sneak attack larger fish. Another one of their behaviors is to mimic a Cleaner Wrasse and when the host fish responds docilely, the blenny bites a piece of flesh from the unsuspecting fish. Saber-tooth Blennies have large teeth and are very territorial. Found most often hovering just above the reef waiting for unsuspecting prey. Sabertooths make their homes in empty worm or gastropod tubes which they enter backwards. Watch for their tiny heads poking out surveying the territory.

DISTRIBUTION: Endemic to Hawaii.

Leopard
Blenny

Pao'okauila

Sabertooth
Blenny

COMMON NAME: Scarface Blenny

SCIENTIFIC NAME: Cirripectes vanderbilti

AVERAGE SIZE: 2-3in.

FAMILY: Blenny - Blenniidae

DIET: Feeds on benthic algae and detritus.

DEPTH FOUND: 2-30+ft.

HABITAT and BEHAVIOR: Very common, but extremely shy. Best observed from a distance of 10-20 feet away. Found secretively resting on the coral and rock. Often overlooked by snorkelers and divers.

DISTRIBUTION: Endemic to Hawaii.

* * * * *

COMMON NAME: Redspotted Sandperch

SCIENTIFIC NAME: Parapercis schauinslandi

AVERAGE SIZE: 3-4in.

FAMILY: Sandperch - Pinguipedidae

DIET: Feeds primarily on small crabs and shrimp.

DEPTH FOUND: 50-100+ft.

HABITAT and BEHAVIOR: Found perched on small rocks in the sand. Usually seen in small groups of 2-6. Uncommon on the reef.

DISTRIBUTION: Found throughout the Indo Pacific.

* * * * *

COMMON NAME: Flagtail or Tilefish

SCIENTIFIC NAME: Malacanthus brevirostris

AVERAGE SIZE: 7-10in.

FAMILY: Sand-Tilefish - Malacanthidae

DIET: Zooplankton.

DEPTH FOUND: 30-70+ft.

HABITAT and BEHAVIOR: Found hovering over sandy patches close to its den. Note the undulating movement this fish makes with its body while hovering. With patience, you can approach within a foot or so. Once threatened, these fish will dart into their burrow. Uncommon in Hawaii.

DISTRIBUTION: Found East Africa and the Red Sea to Hawaii.

Scarface
Blenny

Redspotted
Sandperch

Flagtail
Tilefish

PARROT FISH FACTS

Parrotfish are amongst the largest and most colorful of all the reef fish. Their average size ranges between 10 to 40in. One way to differentiate a parrot fish from most others (excluding the wrasses) is the conspicuous way they use their pectoral fins to swim. Use of the tail for swimming is reserved for emergency power (warp speed). Adult Parrot Fish have fused front teeth that resemble a "Parrot like" beak. This allows the fish to scrape algae from the rocks and coral. As juveniles, their teeth are singular and fuse as they mature. A set of grinding plates located in the back of the fish's mouth grinds the coral until the final result is the fine sand that most of our tropical beaches are made of. One large sized parrot fish can make a ton of sand a year.

At night the Parrotfish often secretes, and sleeps inside, a mucous cocoon for protection from nocturnal predators, such as the moray eel.

Like the Wrasse family the female Parrotfish can change their sex and become supermales that are the largest and most colorful of the species.

COMMON NAME: Bullethead Parrotfish

SCIENTIFIC NAME: Scarus sordidus

AVERAGE SIZE: 10-12in.

FAMILY: Parrotfish - Scaridae

DIET: Feeds on algae and coral.

DEPTH FOUND: 10-100+ft.

HABITAT and BEHAVIOR: As juveniles the Bullethead Parrotfish often schools and lives in shallow lagoons and bays. This fish starts to gain its rainbow-like colors as it matures. The males are the brightly colored of the species, while the females appear a dark purple.

DISTRIBUTION: Throughout the Indo Pacific.

Male
Bullethead
Parrotfish

Uhu

Female
Bullethead
Parrotfish

Uhu

COMMON NAME: Palenose Parrotfish
SCIENTIFIC NAME: Scarus psittacus
AVERAGE SIZE: 9-10in.
FAMILY: Parrotfish - Scaridae
DIET: Feeds on algae and coral.
DEPTH FOUND: 10-100+ft.
HABITAT and BEHAVIOR: Found in a variety of reef habitats from rubble to rich coral gardens. Often observed in mixed schools. Shy upon approach. The males are the brightly colored of the species, while the females appear a dark purple.
DISTRIBUTION: Throughout the Indo Pacific.

COMMON NAME: Stareyed or Bucktooth Parrotfish
SCIENTIFIC NAME: Calotomus carolinus
AVERAGE SIZE: 15-20in.
FAMILY: Parrotfish - Scaridae
DIET: Feeds on leafy and encrusting algae.
DEPTH FOUND: 10-100+ft.
HABITAT and BEHAVIOR: Found in a variety of reef habitats from rubble to rich coral gardens. Take note of the separated front teeth which differs from the fused teeth of the other Parrotfish. The Star-like pattern around the eye is the distinctive feature that makes identification easy. The males are the brightly colored of the species, while the females appear a dark purple.
DISTRIBUTION: Throughout the Indo Pacific.

COMMON NAME: Redlip Parrotfish
SCIENTIFIC NAME: Scarus rubroviolaceus
AVERAGE SIZE: 20-25in.
FAMILY: Parrotfish - Scaridae
DIET: Feeds on algae and coral.
DEPTH FOUND: 10-100+ft.
HABITAT and BEHAVIOR: This is one of the largest of the Hawaiian reef fishes. Redlips inhabit rocky areas with boulders. The males are the brightly colored of the species. Very skittish upon approach.
DISTRIBUTION: Throughout the Indo Pacific.

Palenose
Parrotfish

Uhu

Stareye
Parrotfish

Ponuhunuhu

Redlip
Parrotfish

Palukaluka

SCORPION FISH FACTS

The Scorpionfish family is made up of a diverse number of species, including the Lionfish and Turkeyfish. All fish in this family have many similar characteristics such as: They are all ambush predators that have a venomous dorsal spine for protection. They do not have a gas bladder, which means they sink when they stop actively swimming. As a result, you will usually find them resting on the bottom. The Titan and Devil Scorpionfish have a large head and a stocky body with fleshy appendages that aid in the fishes camouflage.

The venomous dorsal spine is only for protection, if touched it can be deadly to some people. The good news is, Scorpionfish are quite passive to snorkelers and divers. In fact you will have a hard time spotting these masters of camouflage. Just watch where you place your hands and feet.

As ambush predators, Scorpionfish make their living by resting motionless on the bottom, or under a ledge waiting for a bite size creature to swim, or crawl by. These predator are very quick when it comes to ingesting small fish and invertebrates.

COMMON NAME: Leaf Scorpionfish
SCIENTIFIC NAME: Taenianotus triacanthus
AVERAGE SIZE: 2-3in.
FAMILY: Scorpionfish - Scorpaenidae
DIET: Ambush predator who feeds on small crustaceans and fish.
DEPTH FOUND: 5-100+ft.
HABITAT and BEHAVIOR: The Leaf fish uses its color and shape as its primary defense. The dorsal fins of the leaf fish are not a danger to humans. This species is commonly found in shallow surging water and is often observed rocking back and forth to mimic algae in the surge. Colors vary from red, yellow, lime green, and dark brown with speckles, along with many other subtle variations.
DISTRIBUTION: Indo Pacific.

COMMON NAME: Titan Scorpionfish
SCIENTIFIC NAME: Scorpaenopsis cacopsis
AVERAGE SIZE: 15-20in.
FAMILY: Scorpionfish - Scorpaenidae
DIET: Feeds on crustaceans and fish.
DEPTH FOUND: 10-100+ft.
HABITAT and BEHAVIOR: The Titan Scorpionfish is the largest of the Hawaiian species. This is an ambush predator that lies motionless waiting for prey. Due to its excellent camouflage, Titans are easily overlooked. Check under ledges and coral mounds near rubble bottoms.
DISTRIBUTION: Endemic to Hawaii.

Leaf
Scorpionfish

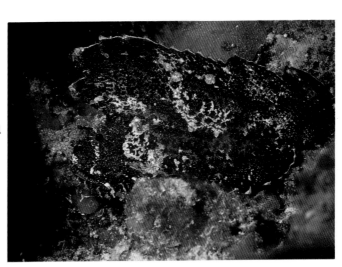

Titan
Scorpionfish

Nohu

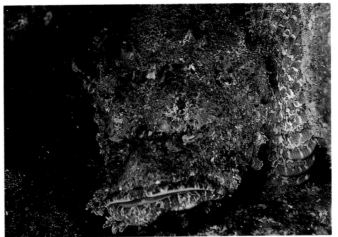

COMMON NAME: Hawaiian Lionfish
SCIENTIFIC NAME: Dendrochirus barberi
AVERAGE SIZE: 4-5in.
FAMILY: Scorpionfish - Scorpaenidae
DIET: Nocturnal feeders who prey on crustaceans and fish.
DEPTH FOUND: 25-100+ft.
HABITAT and BEHAVIOR: Found hiding under ledges or in caverns during the day. Look under coral mounds and up on the ceilings of the caverns and arch ways. Lionfish are shy, but quite approachable, just don't touch them. Their dorsal spine is venomous. The Lionfish will generally stay fairly motionless and passive unless it feels threatened. This species is uncommon.
DISTRIBUTION: Endemic to Hawaii.

*　*　*　*　*

COMMON NAME: Hawaiian Turkeyfish
SCIENTIFIC NAME: Pterois sphex
AVERAGE SIZE: 6-7in.
FAMILY: Scorpionfish - Scorpaenidae
DIET: Feeds on crustaceans and fish.
DEPTH FOUND: 25-100+ft.
HABITAT and BEHAVIOR: Found hiding under ledges or in caverns during the day. Turkeyfish actively feed at night and are found most often on the ceilings of caverns and overhangs. This species is common. You will usually find "horn like" protrusion over the eyes with this species.
DISTRIBUTION: Endemic to Hawaii.

*　*　*　*　*

COMMON NAME: Decoy Scorpionfish
SCIENTIFIC NAME: Iracundus signifer
AVERAGE SIZE: 3-5in.
FAMILY: Scorpionfish - Scorpaenidae
DIET: Feeds on small fish.
DEPTH FOUND: 20-100+ft.
HABITAT and BEHAVIOR: Decoy Scorpionfish are ambush predators that use their dorsal fin as a lure. When hunting they will move their dorsal fin from side to side creating a wavering like motion that gives a very close resemblance to a small fish in motion. This species is often found on sandy, rubble bottoms. Passive upon approach.
DISTRIBUTION: From Hawaii throughout the Central and Eastern Pacific, and the Red Sea.

Hawaiian
Lionfish
Scorpionfish

Hawaiian
Turkeyfish
Scorpionfish

Decoy
Scorpionfish

COMMON NAME: Devil Scorpionfish

SCIENTIFIC NAME: Scorpaenopsis diabolus

AVERAGE SIZE: 10-12in.

FAMILY: Scorpionfish - Scorpaenidae

DIET: Feeds on crustaceans and fish.

DEPTH FOUND: 5-100+ft.

HABITAT and BEHAVIOR: Devil Scorpionfish are ambush predators found most often on sandy, rubble bottoms. Look for a sandy gray colored hump. As the only "Humpback" species in Hawaii the Devil is noted for its ugly face. Close observation reveals if disrupted it will flash its bright colors from the underside of its pectorals as a warning of its presence.

DISTRIBUTION: Found in Hawaii, the Red Sea, Central and Eastern Pacific.

HAWKFISH FACTS

As an ambush predator that lacks a swim bladder, you will usually find Hawkfish resting motionless on the open reef. Hawkfish are very territorial. Most Hawkfish have a small territory within which they have selected 3-4 places they like to perch as they survey the reef. The male is very territorial and generally maintains a harem of females.

With eyes that work independently, Hawkfish are very efficient hunters. They prey on small fish, such as Filefish, and invertebrates.

Reproduction occurs by release and fertilization in the open water where the eggs are carried off into the current.

COMMON NAME: Arc-Eye Hawkfish

SCIENTIFIC NAME: Paracirrhites arcatus

AVERAGE SIZE: 4-5in.

FAMILY: Hawkfish - Cirrhitidae

DIET: Ambush predator who feeds on crustaceans and fish.

DEPTH FOUND: 5-100+ft.

HABITAT and BEHAVIOR: Usually found perched on lobe coral. Lives in bays, lagoons, and seaward reefs. Very common.

DISTRIBUTION: Found throughout the Indo Pacific.

* * * * *

COMMON NAME: Redbar Hawkfish

SCIENTIFIC NAME: Cirrhitops fasciatus

AVERAGE SIZE: 3-5in.

FAMILY: Hawkfish - Cirrhitidae

DIET: Ambush predator who feeds on small crustaceans and fish.

DEPTH FOUND: 15-100ft.

HABITAT and BEHAVIOR: One of the most commonly overlooked fish on the reef. Usually found near the bottom in shallow water.

DISTRIBUTION: Found in Hawaii, Japan, Madagascar, and Mauritius.

Devil
Scorpionfish

Nohu 'omakaha

Arc-Eye
Hawkfish

Pili-ko'a

Redbar
Hawkfish

Pili-ko'a

COMMON NAME: Blackside or Freckled Hawkfish
SCIENTIFIC NAME: Paracirrhites forsteri
AVERAGE SIZE: 6-7in.
FAMILY: Hawkfish - Cirrhitidae
DIET: Ambush predator who feeds on crustaceans and fish.
DEPTH FOUND: 5-100+ft.
HABITAT and BEHAVIOR: Territorial by nature, usually found perched on top of rocks or coral. Located in lagoons and seaward reefs. This species has a haremic sex life. At night Hawkfish rest on the coral in a dormant state at which time their colors will fade.
DISTRIBUTION: Found throughout the Indo Pacific.

COMMON NAME: Longnose Hawkfish
SCIENTIFIC NAME: Oxycirrhites typus
AVERAGE SIZE: 3-5in.
FAMILY: Hawkfish - Cirrhitidae
DIET: Feeds on small planktonic crustaceans.
DEPTH FOUND: 100+ft.
HABITAT and BEHAVIOR: Longnose hawkfish are often associated with Black Coral in Hawaii. Found on current swept, deep water sloping dropoffs. Rarely found above 100ft, Longnoses are common at greater depths.
DISTRIBUTION: Found Indo-Pan-Pacific.

COMMON NAME: Stocky Hawkfish
SCIENTIFIC NAME: Cirrhitus pinnulatus
AVERAGE SIZE: 9-11in.
FAMILY: Hawkfish - Cirrhitidae
DIET: Ambush predator primarily feeding on crabs, crustaceans and fish.
DEPTH FOUND: Surge zone - 50+ft.
HABITAT and BEHAVIOR: The largest of the family found in Hawaii. Often mistaken for a Scorpionfish because of its size, camouflage color, and similar behavior. Found often in very shallow water perched on rocks or coral. Shoreline fishermen report sometimes catching this species.
DISTRIBUTION: Found throughout the Indo Pacific.

Blackside
Hawkfish

Hilu
Pili-ko'a

Long-Nose
Hawkfish

Stocky
Hawkfish

Po'o-pa'a

ANGEL FISH FACTS

Often mistaken for Butterflyfish, Angelfish have few similarities other than shape. The one definitive way to distinguish between the two, is by the spine located on the lower gill plate of all Angelfish.

There are four species of Angelfish in Hawaii all of which are very shy and skittish. Three of the species (Flame, Fishers, and Potters), are found living in small colonies close to the protection of the coral.

The social system of Angelfish seem to be similar to the wrasses haremic system, but on a smaller scale.

The diet of the Angelfish consists of grazing on algae to feeding on small invertebrates.

COMMON NAME: Bandit Angelfish
SCIENTIFIC NAME: Holacanthus arcuatus
AVERAGE SIZE: 5-7in.
FAMILY: Angelfish - Pomacanthidae
DIET: Feeds mostly on sponges.
DEPTH FOUND: 40-100+ft.
HABITAT and BEHAVIOR: Found generally in 60+ feet of water. Since this is a free roaming Angelfish, and the most curious of the Hawaiian Angelfish, it will often approach scuba divers.
DISTRIBUTION: Endemic to Hawaii.

$*$ $*$ $*$ $*$ $*$

COMMON NAME: Fisher's or Dusky Angelfish
SCIENTIFIC NAME: Centropyge fisheri
AVERAGE SIZE: 3in.
FAMILY: Angelfish - Pomacanthidae
DIET: Feeds on filamentous algae.
DEPTH FOUND: 60-100+ft.
HABITAT and BEHAVIOR: This is a fairly uncommon fish to find on the reef. Like most Hawaiian Angelfish it is extremely shy. Usually darting in and out of cover while feeding. Though they have been observed in 40ft of water, Duskys prefer deep water of 80ft or more, and are often found in small colonies of 5-10 fish. This is a very difficult fish to get a close look at due to its extreme shyness.
DISTRIBUTION: Endemic to Hawaii.

Bandit
Angelfish

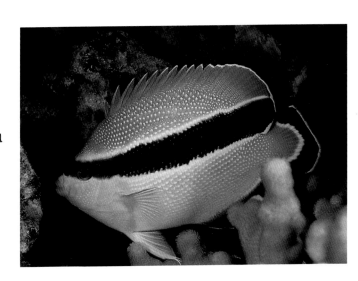

Dusky
Angelfish

COMMON NAME: Flame Angelfish
SCIENTIFIC NAME: Centropyge loriculus
AVERAGE SIZE: 2-3in.
FAMILY: Angelfish - Pomacanthidae
DIET: Feeds on filamentous algae.
DEPTH FOUND: 15-100ft.
HABITAT and BEHAVIOR: Found in areas of rich coral growth. Flame Angelfish like areas that are calm most of the time. This is a very difficult fish to get a good look at due to its shyness. Often observed scurrying in and out of the finger coral. Uncommon in Hawaii.
DISTRIBUTION: Found from Palau to Hawaii.

✳ ✳ ✳ ✳ ✳

COMMON NAME: Potter's Angelfish
SCIENTIFIC NAME: Centropyge potteri
AVERAGE SIZE: 3-5in.
FAMILY: Angelfish - Pomacanthidae
DIET: Feeds on filamentous algae.
DEPTH FOUND: 15-100ft.
HABITAT and BEHAVIOR: The most common of Hawaiian Angelfish. The Potter's is seen busily feeding near the bottom darting in and out of coral cover. Potter's are very shy and difficult to observe up close.
DISTRIBUTION: Endemic to Hawaii.

EMPERORFISH FACTS

These fish are closely related to Porgies, Snappers and Grunts. They have highly developed canine teeth, along with molar type teeth. Also note the thick lips that are characteristic of the species. Generally a very shy fish.

COMMON NAME: Mu Fish or Bigeye Emperor
SCIENTIFIC NAME: Monotaxis grandoculis
AVERAGE SIZE: 20-24in.
FAMILY: Emperors - Lethrinidae
DIET: Feeds on a variety of crustaceans.
DEPTH FOUND: 10-100+ft.
HABITAT and BEHAVIOR: Found schooling well above the reef during the day resting. Mu Fish hunt singularly at night. Upon close observation you will notice Mu Fish have very human like teeth.
DISTRIBUTION: Indo Pacific.

Flame
Angelfish

Potter's
Angelfish

Mu Fish

DAMSELFISH FACTS

Damselfish are a group of small fish that are very territorial. Some Damselfish will actually charge at scuba divers to scare them away from their territory. Fortunately they are so small they cannot possibly harm a human.

Before reproduction takes place, the female Damselfish will prepare a coral or rock area to lay her eggs. Once the eggs are laid the male fertilizes and guards over them until they are "hatched". At this time the damselfish becomes even more aggressive. A prime example of this is the way Sergeant Major Damselfish prepares plate coral and ferociously guards the unhatched eggs. Damselfish feed on zooplankton and algae.

COMMON NAME: Agile Chromis
SCIENTIFIC NAME: Chromis agilis
AVERAGE SIZE: 2-4in.
FAMILY: Damselfish - Pomacentridae
DIET: Feeds on zooplankton.
DEPTH FOUND: 15-100+ft.
HABITAT and BEHAVIOR: Very common on Hawaiian reefs. Found in loosely associated schools. This species locates itself close to the reef for protection. As a scuba diver, if you sit quietly the damselfish will often get curious and closely approach you.
DISTRIBUTION: Indo Pacific.

COMMON NAME: Chocolate-dip Chromis
SCIENTIFIC NAME: Chromis hanui
AVERAGE SIZE: 2-3in.
FAMILY: Damselfish - Pomacentridae
DIET: Feeds on zooplankton.
DEPTH FOUND: 5-100+ft.
HABITAT and BEHAVIOR: Very common on Hawaiian reefs. Found in loosely associated schools. This species is very similar to the Agile Chromis but lacks the pink coloration on it's head and chest. You will find these fish located close to the reef for protection. As a scuba diver, if you sit quietly the damselfish will often get curious and closely approach you.
DISTRIBUTION: Endemic to Hawaii.

Agile Chromis
Damselfish

Chocolate Dip
Damselfish

COMMON NAME: Oval Chromis
SCIENTIFIC NAME: Chromis ovalis
AVERAGE SIZE: 3-5in.
FAMILY: Damselfish - Pomacentridae
DIET: Feeds on copepods, fish eggs and crustacean larvae.
DEPTH FOUND: 20-100+ft.
HABITAT and BEHAVIOR: Common on Hawaiian reefs. This species feeds up in the water column above the reef, but never too far away from a sheltering crevice, or coral head. Like most Damselfish it is very territorial and found in small schools.
DISTRIBUTION: Endemic to Hawaii.

COMMON NAME: Blue-eye Damselfish
SCIENTIFIC NAME: Plectroglyphidodon johnstonianus
AVERAGE SIZE: 3-4in.
FAMILY: Damselfish - Pomacentridae
DIET: Feeds on coral polyps.
DEPTH FOUND: 15-100+ft.
HABITAT and BEHAVIOR: Generally closely associated with Antler or Cauliflower coral. Found actively swimming between the coral branches. Easily approached. Visibly displaying more aggression as divers or snorkelers get closer. Note the blue iris.
DISTRIBUTION: Indo Pacific.

COMMON NAME: Pacific Gregory
SCIENTIFIC NAME: Stegastes fasciolatus
AVERAGE SIZE: 3-5in.
FAMILY: Damselfish - Pomacentridae
DIET: Feeds on filamentous algae.
DEPTH FOUND: 5-30ft.
HABITAT and BEHAVIOR: Found in very shallow water, usually the surge zone. This is one of the most abundant shallow water reef fish in Hawaii. Easy to approach.
DISTRIBUTION: Indo Pacific.

Oval Chromis
Damselfish

Blue-Eye
Damselfish

Pacific Gregory
Damselfish

COMMON NAME: Blackspot Damselfish

SCIENTIFIC NAME: Abudefduf sordidus

AVERAGE SIZE: 3-5in.

FAMILY: Damselfish - Pomacentridae

DIET: Feeds on benthic algae and small crustaceans.

DEPTH FOUND: 5-30ft.

HABITAT and BEHAVIOR: Found in very shallow water, usually in the surge zone. As with most Damselfish the this one is very territorial which makes it very easy to observe and photograph.

DISTRIBUTION: Found throughout the Indo Pacific.

✳ ✳ ✳ ✳ ✳

COMMON NAME: Hawaiian Sergeant Major Fish

SCIENTIFIC NAME: Abudefduf abdominalis

AVERAGE SIZE: 6-9in.

FAMILY: Damselfish - Pomacentridae

DIET: Feeds on zooplankton and algae.

DEPTH FOUND: Surface-90ft.

HABITAT and BEHAVIOR: Found mostly up off the bottom feeding in the water column. One *HABITAT* and *BEHAVIOR* of note is, the way they will school and dominate a territory of plate coral. This species will then prepare a section of coral for the laying of its eggs, and protect them ferociously from predators. Sergeant Majors are very common in Hawaii. Found often in large schools, this species, like most Damselfish, is very territorial, especially while guarding the eggs.

DISTRIBUTION: Endemic to Hawaii.

✳ ✳ ✳ ✳ ✳

COMMON NAME: Hawaiian Whitespot Damselfish

SCIENTIFIC NAME: Dascyllus albisella

AVERAGE SIZE: 3-5in.

FAMILY: Damselfish - Pomacentridae

DIET: Feeds on zooplankton, crabs and shrimp larvae.

DEPTH FOUND: Surface-100+ft.

HABITAT and BEHAVIOR: Found as much as 20ft above the bottom feeding. White spots will often make their home on a coral "island" in the sand, away from the main reef. Antler coral is their favorite protection due to the fact they can hide amongst its branches. As a scuba diver, try sitting motionless and see if the damselfish will get curious and approach you, often this is the case. This is a fairly common fish to find on the reef. Like most Damselfish it is very territorial and found in small schools.

DISTRIBUTION: Endemic to Hawaii.

Blackspot
Damselfish

Kupipi

Sergant Major
Damselfish

Mamo

Whitespot
Damselfish

Alo-il'i

TRIGGERFISH FACTS

Hawaii's most famous fish is a member of this family, the **"Humuhumu-nukunuku-a-pua'a"** otherwise known as the Picasso Triggerfish. The Triggerfish gets its family name from the first dorsal spine that can be lowered and raised, and resembles a trigger. When threatened the Triggerfish will retreat to a nearby hole and use its trigger to wedge itself in.

Triggerfish tend to be territorial and aggressive toward other reef fish. They have very powerful jaws that allow them to feed on sea urchins and crustaceans including lobsters. They feed during the daytime and rest in holes at night.

COMMON NAME: Bluechin or Gilded Triggerfish
SCIENTIFIC NAME: Xanthichthys auromarginatus
AVERAGE SIZE: 6-7in.
FAMILY: Triggerfish - Balistidae
DIET: Feeds on zooplankton.
DEPTH FOUND: 40-100+ft.
HABITAT and BEHAVIOR: Found up off the reef feeding on plankton larvae in water greater than 60ft. This species is often found in small colonies. Bluechins are wary upon approach. The male has the bluechin, females are grey.
DISTRIBUTION: Indo Pacific.

COMMON NAME: Black Durgeonfish
SCIENTIFIC NAME: Melichthys niger
AVERAGE SIZE: 10-12in.
FAMILY: Triggerfish - Balistidae
DIET: Feeds mainly on algae and zooplankton.
DEPTH FOUND: 10-100+ft.
HABITAT and BEHAVIOR: This is a fairly common fish in Hawaii. Found most often up in the water column. When approached they will scurry to a protective hole on the reef.
DISTRIBUTION: Circumtropical. The abundance varies greatly from location to location.

Male
Bluegill
Triggerfish

Female
Bluegill
Triggerfish

Black Durgeon
Triggerfish

Humuhumu-
'Ele-'ele

COMMON NAME: Lagoon Triggerfish
SCIENTIFIC NAME: Rhinecanthus aculeatus
AVERAGE SIZE: 6-7in.
FAMILY: Triggerfish - Balistidae
DIET: Varied diet, anywhere from algae to small shrimp and crabs.
DEPTH FOUND: 0-15ft.
HABITAT and BEHAVIOR: Uncommon on Hawaiian reefs. This species likes shallow protected bays or lagoons. Lagoon Triggers are very territorial, especially when protecting their eggs. This is usually a hard fish to approach on most reefs.
DISTRIBUTION: Indo Pacific.

COMMON NAME: Lei or Whiteline Triggerfish
SCIENTIFIC NAME: Sufflamen bursa
AVERAGE SIZE: 6-7in.
FAMILY: Triggerfish - Balistidae
DIET: Feeds on algae, small invertebrates, sea urchins and fish eggs.
DEPTH FOUND: 10-100+ft.
HABITAT and BEHAVIOR: This is a territorial fish found near the bottom in areas below the surge zone. They feed in areas with rock, rubble and coral mix. Lei Triggerfish will often try to bully divers or snorkelers as they approach by charging at them aggressively and turning away at the last second. This is one of the most common and approachable of the Triggerfish.
DISTRIBUTION: Indo Pacific.

COMMON NAME: Pinktail Durgeonfish
SCIENTIFIC NAME: Melichthys vidua
AVERAGE SIZE: 10-12in.
FAMILY: Triggerfish - Balistidae
DIET: Algae detritus, crabs, shrimp, and small fish.
DEPTH FOUND: 10-100+ft.
HABITAT and BEHAVIOR: This is a common fish often found above the reef in current swept areas in Hawaii. Will usually dive toward shelter upon approach.
DISTRIBUTION: Indo Pacific.

Lagoon Triggerfish

Humuhumu-Nukunuku-A-pua'a

Whiteline Triggerfish

Pinktail Durgeon Triggerfish

Humuhumu-Hi'u-kole

COMMON NAME: Reef or Picasso Triggerfish
SCIENTIFIC NAME: Rhinecanthus rectangulus
AVERAGE SIZE: 7-9in.
FAMILY: Triggerfish - Balistidae
DIET: Varied diet, anywhere from algae to small shrimp and crabs.
DEPTH FOUND: 10-40ft.
HABITAT and BEHAVIOR: Common on Hawaiian reefs, but very skittish. This species is found in the surge zone, likes areas of bare rock, rubble and coral. Feeds throughout the daytime, rests in holes at night.
DISTRIBUTION: Indo Pacific.

TRUNKFISH FACTS

The Trunkfish has a very interesting make up. Its body is actually a shell that has small gaps for its eyes, mouth, gill openings, anus, and caudal peduncle . Trunkfish move slowly and are territorial by nature. In Hawaii the Trunkfish is a subspecies of the ones found throughout the Indo Pacific.

COMMON NAME: Spotted Trunkfish
SCIENTIFIC NAME: Ostracion meleagris
AVERAGE SIZE: 2-4in.
FAMILY: Trunkfish - Ostraciidae
DIET: Feeds mainly on algae, sponges, and mollusks.
DEPTH FOUND: 10-100ft.
HABITAT and BEHAVIOR: This is a fairly common fish in Hawaii. Found most often hiding in the coral crevices. Males are brightly colored with blue sides. Females are brown with white spots. This particular subspecies is unique to Hawaii. Can be curious if approached slowly.
DISTRIBUTION: From Hawaii to the coast of Africa.

Picasso
Triggerfish

Humuhumu-
Nukunuku-
A-pua'a

Male
Trunkfish

Moa

Female
Trunkfish

Moa

PUFFERFISH FACTS

Pufferfish are famous for the way they can draw water into a specialized chamber and inflate their bodies to deter predators from swallowing them. Another observed behavior is, once threatened they may swim into a hole and inflate so that it's impossible to get them out. Pufferfish are relatively slow swimmers and depend on their ability to inflate as their primary defense.

Eating Pufferfish is a delicacy in Japan, but it can have its draw backs. If not prepared just right it becomes deadly. Puffers are extremely toxic to eat unless you know exactly how to prepare them, and even then it is still considered risky. You will find most species of Pufferfish to be common in Hawaii.

COMMON NAME: Ambon Toby or Sharpnose Pufferfish
SCIENTIFIC NAME: Canthigaster amboinensis
AVERAGE SIZE: 3-4in.
FAMILY: Pufferfish - Tetraodontidae
DIET: Feeds on algae, corals, invertebrates, brittle stars and mollusks.
DEPTH FOUND: 10-80ft.
HABITAT and BEHAVIOR: This species covers a fairly large area while feeding. Often found in the surge zone, Sharpnose Puffers are easily approached and will sometimes become curious and approach a diver.
DISTRIBUTION: Indo Pacific.

✳   ✳   ✳   ✳   ✳

COMMON NAME: Crown Toby or Crown Pufferfish
SCIENTIFIC NAME: Canthigaster coronata
AVERAGE SIZE: 3-4in.
FAMILY: Pufferfish - Tetraodontidae
DIET: Feeds on algae and corals. Will also feed on invertebrates, such as brittle stars and mollusks.
DEPTH FOUND: 50-100+ft.
HABITAT and BEHAVIOR: This species favors deeper water than other Puffers, usually observed in 75 feet and deeper. A naturally curious fish.
DISTRIBUTION: Indo Pacific.

Sharpnose
Pufferfish

Crown
Pufferfish

COMMON NAME: Lantern Toby
SCIENTIFIC NAME: Canthigaster epilampra
AVERAGE SIZE: 3-4in.
FAMILY: Pufferfish - Tetraodontidae
DIET: Feeds on algae, corals, and invertebrates.
DEPTH FOUND: 80+ft.
HABITAT and BEHAVIOR: This species is often observed in 80 feet or deeper. Cautious when approached.
DISTRIBUTION: Hawaii to the tropical Western Pacific.

✳ ✳ ✳ ✳ ✳

COMMON NAME: Hawaiian Pufferfish
SCIENTIFIC NAME: Canthigaster jactator
AVERAGE SIZE: 2-3in.
FAMILY: Pufferfish - Tetraodontidae
DIET: Feeds mainly on algae, sponges and mollusks.
DEPTH FOUND: 10-100ft.
HABITAT and BEHAVIOR: Commonly found in Hawaii, this fish can be aggressive towards other small fish or divers, fortunately it's not big enough to threaten humans. This aggressive behavior makes this Puffer easy to observe up close.
DISTRIBUTION: Endemic to Hawaii.

✳ ✳ ✳ ✳ ✳

COMMON NAME: Stripebelly Pufferfish
SCIENTIFIC NAME: Arothron hispidus
AVERAGE SIZE: 14-18in.
FAMILY: Pufferfish - Tetraodontidae
DIET: Has an extremely variable diet. Feeds on brittle stars, algae, starfish, coral and some small crustaceans.
DEPTH FOUND: 10-100ft.
HABITAT and BEHAVIOR: Habitat is as varied as its diet. Found in shallow lagoons to deep current sweep drop offs. Will allow you to approach within a few feet then will flee just far enough away to feel safe.
DISTRIBUTION: Indo Pacific to the Tropical Eastern Pacific.

Lantern Toby
Pufferfish

Hawaiian
Pufferfish

Stripebelly
Pufferfish

Keke

COMMON NAME: Whitespotted Pufferfish
SCIENTIFIC NAME: Arothron meleagris
AVERAGE SIZE: 10-12in.
FAMILY: Pufferfish - Tetraodontidae
DIET: Feeds mainly on coral along with algae sponges and mollusks.
DEPTH FOUND: 10-100ft.
HABITAT and BEHAVIOR: This is a fish that is commonly found singularly in coral grown areas. This Puffer will feed at night, which is a very easy time to approach this fish, (as well as with most fish). When a Whitespotted Puffer feels threatened, it will hide in a hole and puff up to wedge itself in. This is a very effective defense tactic.
DISTRIBUTION: From Hawaii to the coast of Africa.

COMMON NAME: Porcupinefish
SCIENTIFIC NAME: Diodon hystrix
AVERAGE SIZE: 22-25in.
FAMILY: Porcupinefish - Diodontidae
DIET: Feeds mainly on crabs and other small invertebrates.
DEPTH FOUND: 10-100ft.
HABITAT and BEHAVIOR: Found either hiding in caves or under ledges during the day, or free swimming high in the water column. This species forages for food during the night. Porcupinefish are very similar to Puffers, the main difference being their retractable spines. When threatened this species will puff up displaying long spines for defense.
DISTRIBUTION: From Hawaii, Japan and Southern California to Easter Island.

White-Spotted
Pufferfish

'O'opu-hue

Porcupine
Pufferfish

Kokala

FILEFISH FACTS

Filefish are closely related to Triggerfish. They are a shy species that has the ability to change their color pattern to match their surroundings. Due to the fact that Filefish are weak swimmers, they tend to stay relatively close to a home reef. They are best observed foraging for food during the daytime. Their diet consist of coral polyps, algae, and some small crustaceans.

COMMON NAME: Barred Filefish
SCIENTIFIC NAME: Cantherhines dumerilii
AVERAGE SIZE: 10-12in.
FAMILY: Filefish - Monacanthidae
DIET: Branching coral, sea urchins, sponges, mollusks and algae.
DEPTH FOUND: 10-100ft.
HABITAT and BEHAVIOR: This is an common fish found mostly in coral rich bays. Seen swimming in pairs and in an unusual sideways position. Shy upon approach.
DISTRIBUTION: From Hawaii to the coast of Africa.

COMMON NAME: Fantail Filefish
SCIENTIFIC NAME: Pervagor spilosoma
AVERAGE SIZE: 4-5in.
FAMILY: Filefish - Monacanthidae
DIET: Feeds on algae, sponges and shrimp.
DEPTH FOUND: 10-100+ft.
HABITAT and BEHAVIOR: Abundance has varied over the years. This species seems to go through a huge "population explosion" cycle every 40 or so years where they become the most common fish on the reef. This is followed by a massive die off of the majority. The phenomenon was last recorded between 1985-1986. Found mostly in coral rich bays and seen swimming singularly and in pairs. Skittish upon approach.
DISTRIBUTION: Endemic to Hawaii.

Barred
Filefish

O'ili

Fantail
Filefish

O'ili-uwi'uwi

COMMON NAME: Lacefin Filefish
SCIENTIFIC NAME: Pervagor aspricaudus
AVERAGE SIZE: 3-4in.
FAMILY: Filefish - Monacanthidae
DIET: Feeds on algae, sponges and shrimp.
DEPTH FOUND: 5-100ft.
HABITAT and BEHAVIOR: Very similar to the Fantail Filefish in looks and behavior. But Fantails tend to be more colorful and abundant. The Lacefin also has smaller black dots on the end of their body scales. Found near the bottom swimming close to the coral. Difficult to approach.
DISTRIBUTION: Indo Pacific.

$$* \quad * \quad * \quad * \quad *$$

COMMON NAME: Scrolled or Broomtail Filefish
SCIENTIFIC NAME: Aluterus scriptus
AVERAGE SIZE: 20-25in.
FAMILY: Filefish - Monacanthidae
DIET: Feeds on algae, hydrozoans and sea grass.
DEPTH FOUND: 5-100ft.
HABITAT and BEHAVIOR: One of the largest fish found on the reef in Hawaii. Found in a variety of habitats and both in schools or singularly. Reaction to divers varies, generally shy upon approach.
DISTRIBUTION: Circumtropical. From the Great Barrier reef to Hawaii.

MOORISH IDOL FACTS

The Moorish Idol is the only species in its family. They share many of the same characteristics of the Surgeonfish. The Moorish Idols long thin snout allows it to reach into small crevices and pick out food. This fish is a common and generally easy to approach.

COMMON NAME: Moorish Idol
SCIENTIFIC NAME: Zanclus cornutus
AVERAGE SIZE: 7-9in.
FAMILY: Moorish idol - Zanclus cornutus
DIET: Feeds primarily on sponges, also eat other animal and plant life.
DEPTH FOUND: Surge zone - 100+ft.
HABITAT and BEHAVIOR: This is a common species that is often observed feeding under ledges and in crevices. Common to find them in small groups of 3-5.
DISTRIBUTION: Red Sea, the coast of Africa and Indo Pacific to Hawaii.

Lacefin
Filefish

Scrolled
Filefish

Moorish Idol

Kihikihi

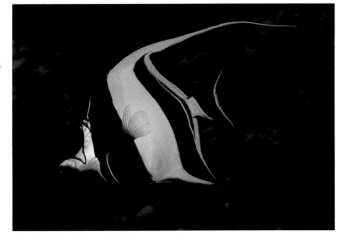

GOBY FACTS

Gobies comprise one of the largest families of fish in Hawaii, but they are seldom observed. This is because they are small and very shy. Most of the Gobies commonly seen in Hawaii live in association with other animals. The Wire Coral Gobies and the Gorgonian Goby being good examples. Both live their lives on a small area of specific coral and divers seldom look close enough to ever spot them. Most gobies are carnivorous and have no gas bladder so they are usually sitting on the bottom, or, as in most cases in Hawaii, on Wire Coral or boat mooring lines.

COMMON NAME: Gorgonian Goby
SCIENTIFIC NAME: Bryaninops amplus
AVERAGE SIZE: 1-2in.
FAMILY: Gobies - Gobiidae
DIET: Feeds on small crustaceans and fish.
DEPTH FOUND: 25-100+ft.
HABITAT and BEHAVIOR: This species lives on whip like corals and can often be found on man made objects such as mooring lines. Seldom noticed by snorkelers and divers. The female of the species will lay an encircling band of eggs on the whip coral, or mooring lines, and in turn the male will guard the eggs until they hatch.
DISTRIBUTION: Indo Pacific.

✳ ✳ ✳ ✳ ✳

COMMON NAME: Wire Coral Goby
SCIENTIFIC NAME: Bryaninops youngei
AVERAGE SIZE: 1in.
FAMILY: Goby - Gobiidae
DIET: Feeds on small crustaceans and fish.
DEPTH FOUND: 15-100+ft.
HABITAT and BEHAVIOR: This is a common species that lives on the wire corals found here in Hawaii. These gobies are seldom noticed by snorkelers and divers due to their small size and ability to blend in with their surroundings. This species usually occurs in pairs. For reproduction purposes this Goby will strip part of the wire coral's tissue away, (usually near the end), so that it can lay its eggs on the coral.
DISTRIBUTION: Indo Pacific.

Gorgonian
Goby

Wire Coral
Goby

GOATFISH FACTS

Goatfish are often found resting in large schools during the day in areas over sand patches. Goatfish are most easily recognized by the two barbels under their chin, which they use as delicate sensors to locate food with. When feeding you will usually find this fish singularly. Some feed by day and night, while other species of goatfish feed only at night. All are common in Hawaii.

COMMON NAME: Blue Goatfish

SCIENTIFIC NAME: Parupeneus cyclostomus

AVERAGE SIZE: 15-18in.

FAMILY: Goatfish - Mullidae

DIET: Daytime feeder on small fish and crustaceans.

DEPTH FOUND: 10-100+ft.

HABITAT and BEHAVIOR: This species is a daytime feeder who uses its barbels to forage for food under coral, or in crevices. Seen often in pairs or small schools. This species is inactive at night and often sleeps in the open on the reef.

DISTRIBUTION: Indo Pacific.

* * * * *

COMMON NAME: Doublebar or Two-barred Goatfish

SCIENTIFIC NAME: Parupeneus bifasciatus

AVERAGE SIZE: 10-12in.

FAMILY: Goatfish - Mullidae

DIET: Feeds on small crustaceans and fish.

DEPTH FOUND: 10-100+ft.

HABITAT and BEHAVIOR: This species forages for food by day and night. Found in a variety of reef habitats, from boulder areas to sandy patches. Distinctive double white bars across the body of this species make it easily identifiable.

DISTRIBUTION: Indo Pacific.

* * * * *

COMMON NAME: Manybar Goatfish

SCIENTIFIC NAME: Parupeneus multifasciatus

AVERAGE SIZE: 5-7in.

FAMILY: Goatfish - Mullidae

DIET: Feeds on small crustaceans and fish.

DEPTH FOUND: 10-100+ft.

HABITAT and BEHAVIOR: This species forages for food by day and is inactive at night. Found most often over sand and rubble areas.

DISTRIBUTION: From Hawaii throughout the Central and Western Pacific.

Blue
Goatfish

Moano Kea

Doublebar
Goatfish

Munu

Manybar
Goatfish

Moana

COMMON NAME: Yellowfin Goatfish

SCIENTIFIC NAME: Mulloides vanicolensis

AVERAGE SIZE: 12-14in.

FAMILY: Goatfish - Mullidae

DIET: Feeds on small fish and crustaceans.

DEPTH FOUND: 40-100+ft.

HABITAT and BEHAVIOR: This species is often found in large schools over sandy patches during the day. At night this species is found singularly over sand and rubble areas foraging for food.

DISTRIBUTION: Indo Pacific.

COMMON NAME: Yellowstripe Goatfish

SCIENTIFIC NAME: Mulloides flavolineatus

AVERAGE SIZE: 12-14in.

FAMILY: Goatfish - Mullidae

DIET: Feeds on small fish and crustaceans.

DEPTH FOUND: 20-100+ft.

HABITAT and BEHAVIOR: Found in the daytime in large schools while resting over sandy patches. This species feeds singularly during the daytime and at night.

DISTRIBUTION: Indo Pacific.

* * * * *

COMMON NAME: Whitesaddle Goatfish

SCIENTIFIC NAME: Parupeneus porphyreus

AVERAGE SIZE: 12-14in.

FAMILY: Goatfish - Mullidae

DIET: Feeds on small crustaceans and fish.

DEPTH FOUND: 10-100+ft.

HABITAT and BEHAVIOR: This is a species that likes deep water. The amount of red coloration seems to be determined by the depth of the individual's habitat. Found often actively feeding in small schools.

DISTRIBUTION: Endemic to Hawaii

Yellowfin
Goatfish

Weke-'ula

Yellowstripe
Goatfish

Weke

Whitesaddle
Goatfish

Kumu

101

SNAPPER FACTS

The Snapper family in Hawaii is poorly represented with only two shallow water species. Both the species were introduced from the Society Islands in the 1950s as a food source. Unfortunately this was unsuccessful.

COMMON NAME: Blacktail or Flametail Snapper

SCIENTIFIC NAME: Lutjanus fulvus

AVERAGE SIZE: 8-10in.

FAMILY: Snappers - Lutjanidae

DIET: Feeds on a variety of crustaceans. Nocturnal.

DEPTH FOUND: 50-100+ft.

HABITAT and BEHAVIOR: Introduced to the Hawaiian waters in 1956 via French Polynesia. Feeds singularly at night. Found schooling up off the reef during the day and resting. Very skittish upon approach. Uncommon.
DISTRIBUTION: Indo Pacific.

$*$ $*$ $*$ $*$ $*$

COMMON NAME: Bluestripe Snapper

SCIENTIFIC NAME: Lutjanus kasmira

AVERAGE SIZE: 8-10in.

FAMILY: Snappers - Lutjanidae

DIET: Feeds on a variety of crustaceans. Primarily nocturnal.

DEPTH FOUND: 30-100+ft.

HABITAT and BEHAVIOR: Introduced to the Hawaiian waters in 1956 via French Polynesia. Feeds singularly at night. This is a very common species, that is found schooling up off the reef, during the day, resting.
DISTRIBUTION: Indo Pacific.

CORNETFISH FACTS

Cornetfish are often mistaken as Trumpetfish. One distinctive difference is the whip like tail vs the fan tail of the Trumpetfish. The color of the Cornetfish is transparent blue to gray. In the daytime this species will often school with others of approximately the same size over sandy, rubble areas. Cornetfish are very aggressive hunters of small fish.

COMMON NAME: Cornetfish

SCIENTIFIC NAME: Fistularia commersonii

AVERAGE SIZE: 33-37in.

FAMILY: Cornetfish - Fistulariidae

DIET: Feeds on small fish and crustaceans.

DEPTH FOUND: 10-100+ft.

HABITAT and BEHAVIOR: This is an ambushfish. Found most often over sandy and rubble areas. Very approachable and curious enough to approach a diver, especially when you are looking away.
DISTRIBUTION: Indo-Pan-Pacific.

Blacktail Snapper

To'au

Bluestripe Snapper

Ta'ape

Cornetfish

GROUPER AND SEA BASS FACTS

Most of the species of Groupers and Basses in Hawaii are found way beyond normal SCUBA diving limits. The most common Grouper, the Peacock grouper, is very shy and difficult to approach. The species of Basslets found here is easy to approach, but uncommon. This family commonly goes through sex reversal, mature females change to males.

COMMON NAME: Bicolor Anthias

SCIENTIFIC NAME: Pseudanthias bicolor

AVERAGE SIZE: 4-5in.

FAMILY: Basslet - Serranidae

DIET: Feeds on zooplankton.

DEPTH FOUND: 70-100+ft.

HABITAT and BEHAVIOR: Uncommon. Found congregated above prominent coral structures feeding in the water column above the coral. Likes deep water current swept areas of 70ft or greater. Harremic sex life.

DISTRIBUTION: Hawaii, New Caledonia and the western Indian Ocean.

$$* \quad * \quad * \quad * \quad *$$

COMMON NAME: Peacock or Blue-spotted Grouper

SCIENTIFIC NAME: Cephalopholis argus

AVERAGE SIZE: 12-15in.

FAMILY: Groupers - Serranidae

DIET: Feeds on fish and crustaceans. Feeds during both day and night.
DEPTH FOUND: 20-100+ft.

HABITAT and BEHAVIOR: Introduced to the Hawaiian waters in 1955 via French Polynesia. Found inhabiting both lagoons and seaward reefs. Feeds singularly at night. Generally skittish with divers and snorkelers.

DISTRIBUTION: Indo Pacific.

SEA CHUB FACTS

The Rudderfish is the most common of the Sea Chubs found in Hawaii. Their natural environment is the shallow surge zone where they school and eat filamentous algae. This fish has also has been observed in large schools where humans feed the fish regularly.

COMMON NAME: Rudderfish

SCIENTIFIC NAME: Kyphosus bigibbus

AVERAGE SIZE: 20-24in.

FAMILY: Sea chubs - Kyphosidae

DIET: Feeds on a variety of filamentous algae.

DEPTH FOUND: Surge zone-100+ft.

HABITAT and BEHAVIOR: Found most of the time in the shallow surging areas. This species is almost always observed in large schools.

DISTRIBUTION: Indo Pacific.

Bicolor Basslet

Peacock Grouper

Rudderfish Sea Chub

FROGFISH FACTS

Frogfish are one of the most difficult of all fishes to locate on a reef. Their porous like skin resembles sponge more than it does fish scales. Anglerfish is another name for the Frogfish due to the "fishing pole" these fish possess. The fishing pole (illicium) has a small, fleshy, piece of "bait" on the end and is used as a lure to attract smaller, curious fish which the Frogfish swallows at lightning speed.

The skin of a Frogfish promotes the growth of algae, which provides camouflage. Frogfish periodically shed the algae growth by replacing their outer skin cells. These fish are able to change colors so as to masterfully match their surroundings. Frogfish are sedentary, but if necessary they can swim along the bottom or even mid-water. Part of their propulsion is accomplished by the use of one small opening behind each pectoral fin. This opening enables the individual to propel water out and functions as a mini "jet" to facilitate their slow and clumsy stumbling across the reef. Frogfish will also use the motion of their tail to move if they desire more speed. Either way it's not fast. Eggs are rafted into a gelatinous mass which is released into the current. Frogfish are often found on the walls of the finger reefs. Usually found in moderate depths, 25-70 ft. As you learn the pattern of the reef you will increase your odds of locating a Frogfish.

COMMON NAME: Frogfish or Anglerfish

SCIENTIFIC NAME: Antennarius commersonii

AVERAGE SIZE: 7-10in.

FAMILY: Frogfish - Antennariidae

DIET: Feeds on fish and crustaceans.

DEPTH FOUND: 10-100+ft.

HABITAT and BEHAVIOR: Ambushfish. Sedentary unless disturbed.

DISTRIBUTION: Indo-Pan-Pacific.

TRUMPET FISH FACTS

The Trumpetfish, a common fish have the ability to change color and will position themselves so as to blend into their surroundings. Trumpetfish use finger coral, sea urchins and other natural objects to hide amongst.

COMMON NAME: Trumpetfish

SCIENTIFIC NAME: Aulostomus chinensis

AVERAGE SIZE: 20-25in.

FAMILY: Trumpetfish - Aulostomidae

DIET: Smaller fish, such as damselfish, surgeonfish and also crustaceans.

DEPTH FOUND: 10-100+ft.

HABITAT and BEHAVIOR: Ambushfish which will often use schools of grazing surgeonfish to provide cover when hunting for prey. Color phases include yellow, uniform brown to green, or mottled brown to green.

DISTRIBUTION: Indo-Pan-Pacific.

Frogfish

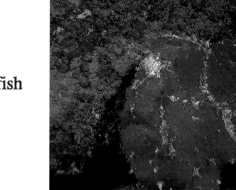

Frogfish

Trumpetfish

Nunu

MORAY EEL FACTS

Moray Eels are very common in Hawaii. They are quite abundant and varied in species. Most are commonly seen while snorkeling or diving. There are a few species, however, that are rare and usually only seen while SCUBA diving, such as the Zebra and Dragon Moray. Moray Eels display a high degree of intelligence, which has been observed in the individuals that have been trained to feed from divers. Some Morays are more aggressive than others, but for the most part they are docile unless provoked or if there is food in the water. Morays do not deserve their fierce "Hollywood" reputation. Contrary to popular opinion, they are *NOT* out *"to get"* unsuspecting divers or snorkelers.

You must realize, however, that if you engage in feeding the eels or fish you increase your odds that you'll get bit. I recommend you refrain from feeding eels, but you decide - it's your fingers. Morays live in the holes and crevices of the reef. They gracefully move their smooth muscular body through the coral crevices, seldom exposing their entire body to the open. It is not unusual to see more than one eel at a time in a hole Eels do occasionally pair up, but for only short periods of time.

Some eels, such as the Zebra and Snowflake Morays, lack the characteristic razor sharp teeth, and instead have crushing teeth used for eating small crustaceans.

COMMON NAME: Yellowmargin Moray

SCIENTIFIC NAME: Gymnothorax flavimarginatus

AVERAGE SIZE: 4ft.

FAMILY: Moray Eel - Muraenidae

DIET: Feeds on small fish and crustaceans.

DEPTH FOUND: 10-100+ft.

HABITAT and BEHAVIOR: This is one of the largest and boldest of the species. Often found with their heads poking out of a hole. Yellowmargins tend to be territorial, some living on the same reef for over 20 years.

DISTRIBUTION: Indo-Pan-Pacific.

$$* \quad * \quad * \quad * \quad *$$

COMMON NAME: Undulated Moray

SCIENTIFIC NAME: Gymnothorax undulatus

AVERAGE SIZE: 3ft.

FAMILY: Moray Eel - Muraenidae

DIET: Feeds on small fish and crustaceans.

DEPTH FOUND: 10-100+ft.

HABITAT and BEHAVIOR: They live in holes or in other areas that provide shelter. This is a common eel that can be very territorial.

DISTRIBUTION: Indo-Pan-Pacific.

Yellowmargin
Moray Eel

Puhi-paka

Undulated
Moray Eel

Puhi-lau-milo

COMMON NAME: Pencil or Dirty Yellow Moray
SCIENTIFIC NAME: Gymnothorax melatremus
AVERAGE SIZE: 10in.
FAMILY: Moray Eel - Muraenidae
DIET: Feeds on crustaceans.
DEPTH FOUND: 10-100+ft.
HABITAT and BEHAVIOR: At first these morays appear to be baby eels, but a full size Pencil moray is only about 10 inches. One of the smallest in the family. Found in cracks and crevices of the reef. Very shy.
DISTRIBUTION: Indo-pan-Pacific.

COMMON NAME: Snowflake Moray
SCIENTIFIC NAME: Echidna nebulosa
AVERAGE SIZE: 25-28in.
FAMILY: Moray Eel - Muraenidae
DIET: Feeds on small fish and crustaceans.
DEPTH FOUND: 10-80ft.
HABITAT and BEHAVIOR: Found in a variety of reef locations. Like most eels, Snowflakes use the cover of the rocks and coral for protection. It is common to find this species in shallow lagoons and even in tide pools.
DISTRIBUTION: Indo-Pan-Pacific.

COMMON NAME: Whitemouth Moray
SCIENTIFIC NAME: Gymnothorax meleagris
AVERAGE SIZE: 2-3 1/2ft.
FAMILY: Moray Eel - Muraenidae
DIET: Feeds on small fish and crustaceans.
DEPTH FOUND: 10-100+ft.
HABITAT and BEHAVIOR: They live in holes or in other areas that provide shelter. This is one of the boldest and most curious of the Morays. Very common at all depth ranges.
DISTRIBUTION: Indo-Pan-Pacific.

**Pencil
Moray Eel**

**Snowflake
Moray Eel**

Puhi-kapa

**Whitemouth
Moray Eel**

Puhi-oni'o

COMMON NAME: Yellow-headed Moray
SCIENTIFIC NAME: Gymnomuraena rueppelliae
AVERAGE SIZE: 2-3ft.
FAMILY: Moray Eel - Muraenidae
DIET: Feeds on crustaceans and small fish.
DEPTH FOUND: 10-100+ft.
HABITAT and BEHAVIOR: Yellow-headed morays are primarily nocturnal and seldom observed during the daytime. Found commonly in lagoons and seaward reefs.
DISTRIBUTION: Indo-Pacific.

✳ ✳ ✳ ✳ ✳

COMMON NAME: Dragon Moray
SCIENTIFIC NAME: Muraena paradalis
AVERAGE SIZE: 3ft.
FAMILY: Moray Eel - Muraenidae
DIET: Feeds on crustaceans and small fish.
DEPTH FOUND: 30-100+ft.
HABITAT and BEHAVIOR: Uncommon and very shy. Dragon morays are noted for the fleshy "horn like" appendages above the eyes and their brilliant colors. One of the least aggressive of the species, the Dragon Moray is often observed in areas of finger coral growth.
DISTRIBUTION: Hawaii to the Mauritius Islands.

COMMON NAME: Zebra Moray
SCIENTIFIC NAME: Gymnomuraena zebra
AVERAGE SIZE: 3ft.
FAMILY: Moray Eel - Muraenidae
DIET: Feeds on crustaceans.
DEPTH FOUND: 10-100+ft.
HABITAT and BEHAVIOR: Zebra eels have small pebble like teeth unlike most other morays. With these specialized teeth they are able to crush the shells of their prey, such as crabs. Zebra morays are shy and uncommon.
DISTRIBUTION: Indo-Pan-Pacific.

Yellowheaded
Moray Eel

Dragon
Moray Eel

Zebra
Moray Eel

Puhi

CONGER EEL FACTS

Conger eels have a comical appearance. Their big lips and pectoral fins, (that look like ears), give them the award for the happiest face underwater. A Conger eel's den can be quite active, with small cleaner shrimp, banded coral shrimp, crabs, and often the remains from last nights dinner. The guests that live in the Conger's hole take advantage of the sloppy eating habits of the eel by feeding on the leftovers, or cleaning up the Conger himself. The shrimp clean the Conger and the Conger provides protection for them. Conger eels have crushing teeth they use to feed on crustaceans. Congers are commonly found in Hawaii.

COMMON NAME: Conger Eel

SCIENTIFIC NAME: Conger cinereus

AVERAGE SIZE: 4ft.

FAMILY: Conger eel - Congridae

DIET: Feeds on crustaceans and small fish.

DEPTH FOUND: 20-100+ft.

HABITAT and BEHAVIOR: Congers like to sleep in holes during the day and feed at night. Generally a curious animal when approached by divers.

DISTRIBUTION: Indo-Pan-Pacific.

FLOUNDER FACTS

Of the 12 species that exist in Hawaii only one is likely to be encountered by divers or snorkelers. While in the larvae phase this fish is symmetrical and has eyes on both sides of its head. As this fish evolves in the planktonic phase, one of their eyes migrates over the top of the head to the other side. By the time the adult Flounder begins its life on the sea bottom it resembles what we see in its mature phase. These fish prefer sandy bottoms where they will often bury themselves up to their watchful eyes in sand while they wait for their unsuspecting prey to wander within striking distance.

COMMON NAME: Peacock Flounder or Manray Flatfish

SCIENTIFIC NAME: Bothus mancus

AVERAGE SIZE: 12-15in.

FAMILY: Flounder - Bothidae

DIET: Feeds on small fish, crabs and shrimp.

DEPTH FOUND: 20-100+ft.

HABITAT and BEHAVIOR: A common fish found burred in the sand Color changes occur as this fish attempts to match the terrain that it is swimming over. Especially noticeable when the flounder moves from a sandy bottom to a coral bottom area.

DISTRIBUTION: Indo Pacific.

Conger
Eel

Puhi-uha

Peacock
Flounder

LIZARDFISH FACTS

Lizardfish are ambush predators that have a reptile look that is used as camouflage to fool prey. The Lizardfish lacks a gas bladder so they must either lie on the bottom or be in motion. They generally live singularly except when mating. Commonly found buried in the sand with only the eyes exposed watching for unsuspecting prey.

COMMON NAME: Variegated Lizardfish
SCIENTIFIC NAME: Synodus variegatus
AVERAGE SIZE: 5-7in.
FAMILY: Lizardfish - Synodontidae
DIET: Feeds on small fish.
DEPTH FOUND: 10-80ft.
HABITAT and BEHAVIOR: These fish are generally found in shallow sandy bottoms of lagoons or seaward reefs. These fish will burrow their body in sand with only head and eyes exposed. Often seen resting on live coral.
DISTRIBUTION: Indo-Pacific.

COMMON NAME: Orangemouth Lizardfish
SCIENTIFIC NAME: Saurida flamma
AVERAGE SIZE: 10-12in.
FAMILY: Lizardfish - Synodontidae
DIET: Feeds on small fish.
DEPTH FOUND: 10-80ft.
HABITAT and BEHAVIOR: These fish are generally found in shallow sandy bottoms of lagoons or seaward reefs. Orange mottling of mouth and head gives this fish its distinctive characteristics.
DISTRIBUTION: Possibly endemic to Hawaii.

Variegated
Lizardfish

'Ulae

Orangemouth
Lizardfish

'Ulae

SQUIRRELFISH FACTS

Squirrelfish feed on crustaceans at night and hide in caves and under ledges during the day. Usually found in schools, these are very common fish seen mostly by SCUBA divers, due to their preference for depths beyond the casual snorkeler.

COMMON NAME: Bigscale Soldierfish
SCIENTIFIC NAME: Myripristis berndti
AVERAGE SIZE: 9-11in.
FAMILY: Squirrelfish - Holocentridae
DIET: Feeds on small crustaceans.
DEPTH FOUND: 45-100+ft.
HABITAT and BEHAVIOR: This is a very common species that is found schooling under ledges, or in caves during the day. At night these fish are actively feeding on crustaceans.
DISTRIBUTION: Indo-pan-Pacific.

* * * * *

COMMON NAME: Hawaiian Squirrelfish
SCIENTIFIC NAME: Sargocentron xantherythrum
AVERAGE SIZE: 5-7in.
FAMILY: Squirrelfish - Holocentridae
DIET: Feeds on small crustaceans.
DEPTH FOUND: 45-100+ft.
HABITAT and BEHAVIOR: Found in schools hiding under ledges or in caves during the day. At night these fish actively feed on crustaceans. The most common of this species. Prefers water depth of 60ft+.
DISTRIBUTION: Indo-Pacific.

Bigscale
Squirrelfish

'U'u

Hawaiian
Squirrelfish

'Ala'ihi

COMMON NAME: Long-jawed Squirrelfish

SCIENTIFIC NAME: Sargocentron spiniferum

AVERAGE SIZE: 12-14in.

FAMILY: Squirrelfish - Holocentridae

DIET: Feeds on small crustaceans.

DEPTH FOUND: 10-100+ft.

HABITAT and BEHAVIOR: Found most often under ledges, in caverns, and around boulders during the daytime. This is the largest of the species. Distinguished by the yellow markings on the pelvic fins on the fish's underside. Long-jaws actively feed at night on crustaceans and small fish.

DISTRIBUTION: Found from the Red Sea to Hawaii and throughout the Central Pacific.

COMMON NAME: Shoulderbar Soldierfish

SCIENTIFIC NAME: Myripristis kuntee

AVERAGE SIZE: 5-7in.

FAMILY: Squirrelfish - Holocentridae

DIET: Feeds on small crustaceans.

DEPTH FOUND: 20-100+ft.

HABITAT and BEHAVIOR: This species is less reclusive than other Squirrelfish, and are often seen on the open reef during the day in large schools. At night these fish actively feed on crustaceans.

DISTRIBUTION: Indo-pan-Pacific.

COMMON NAME: Tahitian or Blue Lined Squirrelfish

SCIENTIFIC NAME: Sargocentron tiere

AVERAGE SIZE: 8-10in.

FAMILY: Squirrelfish - Holocentridae

DIET: Feeds on small crustaceans.

DEPTH FOUND: 10-100+ft.

HABITAT and BEHAVIOR: An uncommon species in Hawaii, found under ledges, in caverns, and around boulders close to the shore line. Distinguished by the faint blue stripes along the center of its scales. This species roams the reef at night in search of crustaceans and small fish.

DISTRIBUTION: Found throughout the Central Pacific to East Africa.

Long-Jawed
Squirrelfish

Shoulderbar
Squirrelfish

'U'u

Tahitian
Squirrelfish

'Ala'ihi

BIGEYEFISH FACTS

The eye of this species is well adapted for nocturnal feeding. Bigeyes are found in caves during the day, and feed at night on large zooplankton, (such as larval fish, crabs, and other crustaceans larvae). There are four species found in Hawaii, of that, only two are found in shallow water where divers and snorkelers can observe them.

COMMON NAME: Glasseye

SCIENTIFIC NAME: Heteropriacanthus cruentatus

AVERAGE SIZE: 10-12in.

FAMILY: Bigeyefish - Priacanthidae

DIET: Zooplankton (such as larval fish, crabs and other crustacean larvae).

DEPTH FOUND: 20-100+ft.

HABITAT and BEHAVIOR: Found in the caves in the daytime and feeding up in the water column at night. Coloring is variable from silvery pink to solid red with silver mottling.

DISTRIBUTION: Circumtropical.

COMMON NAME: Hawaiian Bigeye

SCIENTIFIC NAME: Priacanthus meeki

AVERAGE SIZE: 10-12in.

FAMILY: Bigeyefish - Priacanthidae

DIET: Zooplankton (such as larval fish, crabs, and other crustacean larvae).

DEPTH FOUND: 20-100+ft.

HABITAT and BEHAVIOR: Found in the caves in the daytime and feeding up in the water column at night. This species is bright red.

DISTRIBUTION: Endemic to Hawaii.

Glasseye

'Aweoweo

Hawaiian
Bigeye

'Aweoweo

INDEX of COMMON NAMES

INDEX of SCIENTIFIC NAMES

Hawaiian Invertebrates

Invertebrates are animals that do not posses a backbone. This section includes the invertebrates most commonly seen on Hawaiian reefs, as well as a few unusual, rare species (R). Both the Common Names and Scientific Names are included along with the average length in inches. Most of the featured species are very fragile and some are venomous (V). To protect yourself as well as the creatures, please do not touch the animals.

Freckled Sea Star
Linckia multifora- 6"

Crown-of-Thorns (V)
Acanthaster planci-12"

Pincushion Sea Star
Culcita novaeguineae-10"

Slate Pencil Urchin
Heterocentrotus mammillatus-10"

Sputnik Urchin
Prionocidaris hawaiiensis-10"

Rockboring Urchin
Echinometra mathaei-3"

Spiny Urchin (V)
Echinothrix diadema-11"

Mottled Cucumber
Bohadschia paradoxa-15"

Black Cucumber
Holothuria atra-12"

Christmas Tree Worm
Spirobranchus giganteus-3/4 "

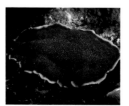
Yellow-Margin Flatworm
Pseudocerus ferrugineus-3"

Zebra Flatworm
Pseudocerus zebra-2"

Freckled Nudibranch
Phyllidiella pustulosa-1 1/2"

Fried-Egg Nudibranch
Phyllidia varicosa-2"

Gold-Lace Nudibranch
Halgerda terramtuentis-1"

Fairy Nudibranch
Pteraeolidia ianthina-4"

Spanish Dancer
Hexabranchus sanguineus-12"

Spanish Dancer Eggs-4"

Vibrating Nudibranch (R)
Chromodoris vibrata-1"

Reticulated Cowry
Cypraea maculifera-2,5"

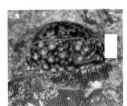
Tiger Cowrie
Cyprae tigris-5"

Cone Shell (V)
Conus pulicarius-1,5 "

Helmet Shell
Cassis cornuta-12"

Pimpled Basket
Nassarius papillosus-2"

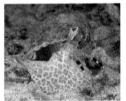
Triton's Trumpet
Charonia tritonis-15"

Octopus
Octopus cyanea-20"

Harlequin Shrimp (R)
Hymenocera picta-1"

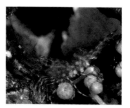  

Reef Shrimp	Wire Coral Shrimp	Scarlet Lady Shrimp
Rhynchocinetes sp.-1 1/2"	*Pontonides unciger*-1/2"	*Lysmata amboinesis*-1 1/2"

Barber Pole Shrimp	Spiny Lobster	Hawaiian Reef Lobster
Stenopus hispidus-2"	*Panulirus penicillatus*-16"	*E. occidentalis*-8"

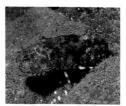 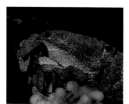 

Sculptured Slipper Lobster	Shovelnose Slipper Lobster	Mole Lobster (R)
Parribacus antarcticus-8"	*Scyllarides squammosus*-11"	*Palinurella wieneckii*-6"

Spider Rock Crab	7-11 Crab	Anemone Hermit Crab
Percnon planissimum-3"	*Carpilius maculatus*-5"	*Dardanus pedunculatus*-4"

Hairy Hermit Crab	Orange-Banded Hermit Crab	Hawaiian Swimming Crab
Aniculus maximus-15"	*Trizopagurus strigatus*-3"	*Charybdis hawaiiensis*-4"

128